# GODDESS WITH MANY FACES

## DISCOVER YOUR ARCHETYPES TO TRANSFORM YOUR LIFE

### SZE WING VETAULT

Published by Poppins House Publishing

www.SzeWingVetault.com

This is a work of non-fiction. The events and conversations in this book have been set down to the best of the author's ability, although some names and details have been changed to protect the privacy of individuals.

Copyright © 2018 by Sze Wing Vetault

All rights reserved. No part of this book may be reproduced or used in any manner without written permission of the copyright owner except for the use of quotations in a book review. For more information, email info@goddessarchetypes.com

First edition October 2018

Aromatherapy appendix by Salvatore Battaglia
www.perfectpotion.com.au

Book edited by Monique Perrine
www.nettlesoup.com.au

Book cover design by Suzana at LSD Design

Goddess Archetype Images by Karen Koski
www.whimicalmuse.com

Typesetting and e-book formatting by Book Cover Cafe
www.bookcovercafe.com

ISBN
978-0-646-99016-3 (paperback)
978-0-6484231-0-2 (ebook)

# Contents

| | |
|---|---:|
| Goddess with Many Faces | v |
| Wisdom of Myths | xxi |
| 1 Athena | 1 |
| 2 Artemis | 20 |
| 3 Demeter | 37 |
| 4 Persephone | 55 |
| 5 Hera | 72 |
| 6 Aphrodite | 90 |
| Emerging as a Goddess | 105 |
| Next Steps | 139 |
| Endnotes | 141 |
| Appendix 1: Aromatherapy and the Goddesses | 143 |
| References | 154 |
| About Sze Wing | 157 |
| Acknowledgement | 158 |

# Goddess with Many Faces

## Discover your archetypes to transform your life

*To know others is wisdom;
To know yourself is enlightenment
To master others requires force;
To master yourself requires true strength.*
**– Lao-tzu, Tao-te Ching**

Not long ago I was at a dinner party and I sat beside the husband of a friend. In the course of our conversation he asked me what I was working on at the moment. I was unsure if this was just a polite question, so I simply said "I am writing a book about women." My dinner companion looked curious and waited for a longer answer, so I went on. "I am writing a book to empower women. I'm using goddess myths, archetypes and the Hero Journey to inspire women in transitions." Perhaps I surprised him, because he then asked, "How did you come up with that idea?" I paused. I thought about it for a moment and said, "I think it has always been there inside me. One day, everything just came together."

Perhaps this is something that has always been there inside all women. Every woman has a story to tell. More importantly, women feel a need to speak about what matters to us, to express our creativity, to activate our passion, to actualize our potentials and to embody the power of a goddess. So often we feel we need permission and courage to say out loud that this is important for us and it is something we care deeply about. We long for a like-minded sisterhood and desire to achieve something great in our time.

In the last few years, a lot has happened that leads me to look more closely at my life as a daughter, wife, mother, friend and career woman. Collectively, a lot has happened in the world regarding women too. We hear stronger voices advocating pay equality and respectful treatment for women. We see a growing number of female leaders in business, media and politics. We feel the need and the urge to rise and claim our power, not just externally, but internally as well.

Women in the Western world may have claimed more rights than our great-grandmothers and the women who came before us in most parts of the world, but centuries of social conditioning have inevitably influenced our unconscious minds about our roles and capabilities in the world.

However this wasn't always the case. Ancient myths originating from a matriarchal period often portray the image of the goddess as the earth's mother, who is powerful and nurturing. When the patriarchal culture took over, the image of the goddess in Greek mythology evolved to sit beside the gods or beneath them as one of their many wives, consorts or mistresses. It was like a shadow was cast over women's psyches, changing our narrative about who we are and why we are here.

Now it is time for women to step out of that shadow and to shine the light within us. Not only are we encouraged to achieve outer success and become influential in the world's affairs. We are also called to emerge as goddesses from within, where our hearts become fearless to love and our minds are inspired to soar.

# Goddess Archetypes

Archetypes are universal patterns of character and experience. They tell us about our strengths and weaknesses; light and shadow; power and vulnerability. We find different archetypes active in us reflecting our many facets as we go through different phases in life.

The goddess is a mystical, feminine archetype that exists within all women. She takes many forms, and her image has evolved through time alongside the changing role and status of women. Goddess wisdom, however, has never faded as it has been carried through the goddess myths, which relate the stories of the goddess archetypes.

Myths are essentially human projections of fear, hope and desire. Despite the technological advancement of the last two millennia, the nature of our fear and love has not changed. That is why myths are powerful and they endure through time. We find common themes across different cultures and geographies. Myths provide us with an understanding of human nature, moral values, social structures and spiritual beliefs. They serve as inspirational stories or cautionary tales. I am drawn to using goddess myths and goddess archetypes because I feel as women we can relate to them personally.

There is a fundamental dynamic behind the behaviour of each goddess archetype which makes her unique. Part of it seems to be innate but part of it is shaped by our social environment.[1] We can be wise and strong like the Greek goddess Athena, or courageous and focused like Artemis. We have the ability to gestate and nurture like Demeter, and we also have alchemical power and divine beauty within us like Aphrodite. Each aspect of the goddess archetype provides us with an opportunity to grow and become the women we are meant to be.

Our identity is reflected in what we do, or are capable of doing. In Mahatma Gandhi's words, 'A man is but the product of his thoughts. What he thinks, he becomes'. If we inhabit our space with love instead of fear, the actions we take will reflect that love. Understanding who we are, and who we aspire to become, will set us on a very different trajectory than the one we would travel without a higher direction.

# The Heroine Journey

Looking back at my younger self, I realise it took me a long time to discover where my true north lay, but some of the Athena archetype attributes were natural to me. I left Hong Kong at sixteen to study in Norway, then London for many years. My worldly ambition took me wherever I could stretch my horizons. Homesickness was never my problem, but it felt almost too cold to admit that. My focus was outward oriented. I wanted to make a difference in the world, but I had no clear vision of what to do or how to do it. I liked the idea of dreaming big and flying high but I had no anchor to ground my ambitions. Fast-forward ten years, with a few life lessons learned through joy and through pain, something shifted in me when I settled in Australia. I am still clearly an extrovert but I have started to feel the gravitational pull toward a more reflective and inward focus. This change transpired through many years of learning from different spiritual teachers and authors. My focus has moved from trying to make a dent in the world toward a desire to connect with people and experience inner worlds. The influence of Aphrodite slowly activated in me as I became

drawn to human potential and how to create transformative experiences for myself and others. I felt inspired to share what I learned and eventually became a coach to support women, men and purpose-driven businesses.

The next big shift came last year when I became a mother. Although I still run my household in a highly organized way, like Athena, and my interest in working with people never faded, I can see how I took on Demeter qualities in my everyday life. The love for my daughter is infinite and my willingness to care for her surprises me. That girl who never felt homesick is gone. I have roots now. I have become far more compassionate for all sentient beings since I have given birth to life myself. I have more courage to let my heart open and be vulnerable, I have more faith to stand by my convictions and I have more strength to show up fully for my life. I know now I have grown into a different woman than I used to be.

Like me, every woman goes through several transitions in life, both biological and psychological. Each transition is ultimately a call to her Heroine Journey, an inner and outer transformation. Many readers are perhaps familiar with the term Hero Journey, coined by the famed mythologist Joseph Campbell. In this book, I will use the term Heroine Journey as we consider examples of women's myths. Your Heroine Journey will likely be quite different from mine. Although there are some transitions that are familiar to all of us. For example, a young girl comes of age and becomes a woman then, sometimes, a mother. Eventually she becomes physically older and hopefully mentally wiser. Alongside these biological life stages, other situations can send women into transition, such as leaving home to live independently, entering or leaving the workforce, marriage, divorce, relocation, changes in their children's lives, career changes or starting a business. The possibilities for change are endless as long as we live. All these transitions are invitations to transform and evolve. With different archetypes active in us, we respond very differently to each transition. Some archetypes get activated while some step back. Therefore, each woman's willingness to look at who she is, identify the archetypal forces active within her, and, most importantly, the strength of her willingness to change, will shape the person she will ultimately become.

## All we need is a miracle

Some people think we can change the world by doing things differently, or by ceasing to do some things altogether. This is an illusion. At best, that can only alleviate some of the symptoms of a problem, new ones will surface before long. Changing the effect will not change the cause. It is cause-and-effect, not the other way round. Who we are governs what we do. The late spiritual teacher and author Dr. Wayne Dyer used to say, 'What comes out when you squeeze an orange? Orange juice of course!' No magical formula, strategy or solution will get us anywhere unless the person who uses them is in alignment with his or her true self. Someone who wants to avoid responsibility may say 'The end will justify the means', while Gandhi believed in 'The end is inherent in the means'. Everything we do is infused with our consciousness. Therefore, to truly change the world, we need to change the way we think, which will change the way we see things.

In any situation when love is withheld or taken away from us or others, it is an invitation for love. 'Things' in life don't happen to us randomly, they happen so that we are called to evolve with higher consciousness, to shift our perception from fear to love, to allow a miracle to happen. In *A Course In Miracles*, the first principle[2] says 'There is no order of difficulty in miracles.' All that matters is the willingness to see things differently, the willingness to change and transform within. The problem many of us have is resistance to change. For a goddess archetype such as Hera, who places a high importance on being married and loyal, sometimes the truly

loving response to a dysfunctional relationship is to end it. For a burnt-out Demeter, who has been tirelessly looking after others and neglecting her own health, the loving response is to stop over-giving and create more balance in her life. Love sometimes says yes, but sometimes it also says no.

When we become aware of our archetypes, in particular our shadow tendencies, we improve our understanding of why we find it hard to say no, or to let go of certain aspects in our lives. It becomes easier to detach ourselves from these tendencies, once we own them and become responsible for them. As for relationships, it becomes easier to see the perspectives of others. Once again, when you change, you see things differently. It is about embracing the inner change so that we can emerge with the outer change. The ultimate purpose of a Heroine Journey is not reaching the summit or conquering the dragon. It is transforming from fear to love and hence empowering the person within. And that is the miracle that can naturally happen to all of us, if we are willing to go for it.

This book hopefully can serve as a conduit for this change to happen, by introducing you to the goddess archetypes, mythical wisdom and spiritual concepts that work together to guide you like a map and compass on your own Heroine Journey.

# Feminine power

Before we set sail to our journey, we must get acquainted with the engine of our ship. All women are unique but we have one thing in common. We have the divine feminine transformative power within us, and that is what connects us with these goddesses. In Sanskrit this power is called *Shakti*. The female principle of divine energy. This energy is creative, vibrant, cosmic and eternal. It empowers us to seek meaning and fulfilment in life. No matter your age, race, marital

status, profession, culture or belief system, you can fully embrace this feminine power. Author and renowned spiritual teacher Marianne Williamson wrote "Feminine power isn't something we go out and acquire; it's already within us. It's something we become willing to experience. Something to admit we have."[3].

This power ignites us, allowing us to shine with our unique light and become the greatest version of ourselves. We can also empower one another: women empowering women. We are living at a time when women have more freedom and opportunity to inspire, to influence and to lead than ever before. However, we are not all enlightened 'goddesses' already, sometimes what we need is a gentle push from the angels, or a voice to tell us we can do it. I know this because I was on the edge for years before I took my own leap of faith.

About a decade ago I was living in a bubble. I was in a relationship with a charming and successful man who recovered from a cocaine addiction but later became a closet alcoholic. At first I didn't know about the drinking problem, but when it got worse, I resisted acknowledging it. Deep down I knew the relationship was dysfunctional, between all the lies and fights, life was comfortable but empty. I thought life was manageable and under control. But as it turned out, it was full of deceit that I managed to ignore. It was my responsibility to live with integrity and authenticity. My denial of the problem was also part of the problem.

Then one day I was confronted by fate. I received a phone call from a devastated woman who had just learned her boyfriend had been unfaithful to her. More disturbingly, she had just realised that she was his so-called 'overseas girlfriend', the other woman. To this day, I am still surprised by my first response, I calmly said "So I guess I must be his Sydney girlfriend then". Her cry on the phone saddened me, not because this discovery would mean the end of my relationship, but because of her tears, her broken heart. I felt her pain and disappointment. Part of me was hurting because of his betrayal, but the other part of me was weeping for her too. Perhaps unconsciously I had known the relationship was coming to an end for some time. I was emotionally prepared for that, but I wasn't prepared to share tears with the other woman in the failed relationship. So there I was, when my second surprise came out of my mouth. I said, "You didn't know. This is not your fault. You can get through this. You deserve the truth and someone better". I felt deeply at that moment how we women must support one another. We understand each other. We know the pain. We know what needs to be said. We lean on one another until we find strength in our own legs.

In truth, there are no failed relationships. There are always lessons to be learned from each one and I wouldn't have met my husband if that relationship had not ended. I wouldn't have moved to another area, met new friends and begun a new chapter in my life.

Looking back, that phone call was one of my quantum moments. It felt timeless and divine. I knew it was a pivotal point in my life. During that couple of years, I was wondering a lot about the meaning and purpose of my life. I felt stuck, dull and longed for inspiration. Now I know the whole ending of the relationship was a call for change and I was the reluctant Heroine who refused to answer the call at first.[4] It still amuses me that it was literally a phone call I answered that changed my life.

I know every woman has her own story, and not only can we learn from each other, but we can empower one another with our own stories, unique gifts, talents and life experiences to fully embrace our feminine power.

In the last five years, since I began coaching and speaking to women on many different platforms, I have not met a single woman who does not feel this feminine power within her, each woman knows she has something unique to offer to this world. It takes courage and commitment to show up and answer that inner calling. But those who have taken that leap of faith have soared. They ignite as they are connected to their inner power. They have found their authentic success in work, blossomed in their relationships and generally thrived in life. If I didn't answer my call, I would not have had the opportunity to meet and work with many inspiring women. I would not have met my husband, or been blessed by our daughter. Even if the universe had contrived for me to meet my husband in some other way, I wouldn't be the same woman that learned and healed from my previous relationship. My husband probably wouldn't even have liked me. No one knows. But I do know that if I didn't take that leap, I wouldn't be able to write this book about goddess archetypes as a toolkit for you to navigate your own Heroine Journey.

# How this book is organized

Throughout this book, you will discover the archetypes you were born with or have cultivated through maturity and life circumstances. You will learn more about different aspects of the archetypes, their tendencies with relationships and career aspirations. You will start to have a better understanding of your inner patterns and how to create changes from within to bring about changes in your outer reality. This transformation can take place no matter where and when you are in life, as long as you are willing and committed to personal growth.

To prepare us for our Heroine Journey, we will first pick up some tools and concepts. In chapter two we will cover the connection between archetypes and our conscious and unconscious minds. We will look at what myths represent in our culture, and what we can learn from them. In the following six chapters (Chapters 3–8), I will introduce six major Greek goddess archetypes that are the most common among us. These chapters will examine *who we are* and perhaps what influences *who we want to become*. I will present the most significant myths for each of the goddesses to exemplify their individual characters and discuss the forms of these archetypes in modern society and how they relate to one another. For example, a headstrong, smart and career-focused Athena archetype may have a very different relationship with her daughter when compared to a Demeter archetype who is a born nurturer and full of maternal instincts. We will look at the 'light' and 'shadow' aspects of each archetype and how they tend to grow as we mature with age or life experience.

Each chapter on the goddesses will conclude with a practical self-care guide including reflective questions and wellness practices to bring more balance in your physical, emotional and spiritual wellbeing. One of my favourite tools to nurture and heal is aromatherapy. It is a holistic approach to personal wellbeing, to revitalise and harmonise the body, mind and spirit. The aromatherapy section in each of the practical goddess wellness guides and the Appendix *Aromatherapy and the Goddesses* are written by Salvatore Battaglia, the founder of *Perfect Potion* (www.perfectpotion.com.au) and the author of *The Complete Guide of Aromatherapy*, now in its third edition, and the forthcoming book *Aroma Tree*.

In the soon to be published book *Aroma Tree*, Battaglia examines the mythology and symbolism associated with each part of the *Aroma tree* – the roots, wood, resin, flowers, leaves fruit and seeds.

In chapter nine, after learning about *who we are* with the goddess archetypes, we will get on to look at *where we are* on our journey. We will unpack the concept of the Heroine Journey and how it may appear in your life. In a typical myth, the Heroine undertakes a mission to find the treasure or slay the dragon in order to save a loved one or the entire world. In our 'personalized' myth, our quest is perhaps to create a meaningful career or to find true love. Whatever it is, it is a call to adventure externally, as well as an opportunity for personal growth internally. I will look at the key adventure stages and what kind of help may greatly affect the outcome of our quest.

After learning about *where* we are in life, we will turn to *when* we are in life. I will examine the idea of the Women's Cycle of Life. Similar to the four seasons in nature, women go through seasons in life. Instead of the well-known notion of the triple goddess: Maiden, Mother and Crone, I will look at the four maturity stages as Maiden, Mother, Matriarch and Wise Woman. In today's world, we see the growing number of female CEOs, politicians and thought leaders; the impactful years of women's lives have significantly increased. Women past their mid-life have a lot to offer the world, in fact, this period may be their golden years, with their accumulated wisdom and resources. I will expand on the shift of archetypal influences as we mature and look at how to manage the change in seasons and social perceptions.

To close this book, we will focus on how to emerge as a powerful modern-day goddess, fully embodied with the divine feminine energy. We will look at how to bring more harmony and peace within ourselves. Women now have more choices in life than ever, however, such opportunities also bring challenges.

For example, how to balance work and family life, which means letting go of the energy of Athena at work to become more like Demeter at home. Another big challenge for many women is to reconnect to their bodies, to reignite their sensual self after a long day of work or, in some cases, years of disconnection between the head and the heart. I will look at how to put all the lesson in this book together to cultivate a more balanced and fulfilling life.

## THE PATH LESS TRAVELLED

If we know our strengths and weaknesses, we can stop ourselves from doing things that we will regret or stop ourselves from making the same mistake twice. Instead we can start to know what truly matters to us. It is often not 'doing' and 'getting', but 'being' that truly matters. We are meant to shine brightly and live purposefully.

Discovering your active goddess archetypes and knowing your unconscious repetitive patterns, brings you more clarity and courage. It also brings you more understanding and acceptance of those around you and your relationships with them.

The moral lessons from the myths, and the 'aha' moments gained from the reflective questions and practical exercises in this book, will naturally inspire you to create a unique and authentic life for yourself. A life that transcends mere physical fulfilment, enriched with spiritual enlightenment as well. That is what it is to live your personal myth, a life that is filled with insights and integrated with wisdom.

Since the day I began my own Heroine Journey, and through a decade of research, learning, coaching and teaching, I have seen first-hand how much change and growth have came into my life. I have found love and peace. I have become a wife and a mother, a better daughter and friend, a more humble teacher and student. If I had a chance to talk to my younger self, I would whisper to her to live with less fear and more faith. Fewer 'what-ifs' but more 'what-elses'. Since I cannot talk to my younger self, I pour my heart and mind into creating this book for you. This book will not provide you with all the answers, but it is my hope that it will prompt you to ask yourself some questions that really matter.

It is my vision that when you pick up this book, even just to open a page or read a sentence, you will have somehow answered the call that came from deep within your unconscious. It is like your radar has finally picked up a signal, and we can hear the beeping sound going in the background. You have just embarked on a transformative journey, a quest for a more meaningful and connected life. This quest is not always a walk in the park with the perfume of roses in the air. At times, you will be confronted by the dark night of the soul, or lead into uncharted territory. But there will also be times when you feel blessed and aided by the goddesses. Whenever your faith wavers, you can lean on mine. Not only because I have faith in you, but I also have deep faith in the greater power of this universe.

Regardless of what may come along the road, it will be *your* path, a path that is less travelled and the reward will be far more than just reaching your intended destination. Unexpected gifts await you along the way.

So, I say, my dear friend, go forth with courage and go forth with grace. With an open heart and willing mind, step into your Age of Wisdom now.

# WISDOM OF MYTHS

*Myths are public dreams; Dreams are private myths*
– Joseph Campbell

*Nights through dreams tell the myths forgotten by the day.*
– **Carl G. Jung**

## DREAMS AND MYTHS

Since the end of my dysfunctional relationship over a decade ago, I began to read books on body-mind connections and spirituality. I took courses and trips overseas to learn from some of the authors directly. I learned exactly what was meant by the saying 'when the student is ready, the teacher will appear'. (Interestingly, I find this true the other way around as well.) Apart from reading and learning daily, I also began to meditate regularly. Shortly after that I started to have vivid dreams at night. Many times it was like watching a medieval movie, but I was the main character in it. When I woke in the morning, I remembered how everything looked: the symbols, clothes, buildings, places and people in my dreams. These dreams also delivered messages, but I did not understand them. As Joseph Campbell puts it, myths are *"the wisdom of deep mysteries of life"*[5]. I felt my dreams held clues to heal my life, and so I began to look at the connections between dreams and myths in more detail.

As my dreams were set in medieval times, I looked up the Arthurian legends and in particular the themes and characters that matched my dreams. These myths opened up a gate of fascination and intrigue in me. The myths of the Lady of the Lake resonated with me greatly, especially the ones related to her giving the magical sword Excalibur to King Arthur and taking the wounded king to his final healing place in Avalon. She reminded me of a goddess figure who guided me in my dreams. She was my wise counsel, who brought light to illuminate the dark, and she lead me on different paths. With her presence, there could be no false pretense or going backwards. To me, she represented divine feminine power, hope and fate. My dreams were telling me to break from the past with courage, become the person I needed to be and to create my new kingdom.

In the words of Joseph Campbell, the most celebrated mythologist, *"Dream is the personalized myth, myth the depersonalized dream"*[6]. Myths carry our projections but depersonalize them in a way that our conscious can accept and process. Among all the myths and fairy tales there is always one or two that particularly capture your heart. They anchor in you because the theme or the lesson of the myth speaks to your unconscious, it carries the message that you really need to hear.

# Unveiling Our Unconscious

In his autobiography, the renowned Swiss psychiatrist Carl G. Jung said *"Everything in the unconscious seeks outward manifestation, and the personality too desires to evolve out of its unconscious conditions and to experience itself as a whole"*[7]. Knowingly or not, we all want to live our life fully, deeply and truthfully. Understanding our unconscious plays a crucial part in knowing who we are. And without knowing who we are, we certainly cannot know the greatness that we are able to become or the legacy we can leave behind, which is our personal myth.

Two of the most fundamental concepts Jung proposed in psychology are the collective unconscious and archetypes. Archetypes, in his words, are *"identical psychic structures common to all"*[8] which together constitute *"the archaic heritage of humanity"*.[9] In other words, he perceived archetypes to be innate psychic structures which have the capacity to initiate, control and mediate the common behavioural characteristics and typical experience of all human beings. We are born with certain archetypes, they are already in our nature, but through personal life experience, the archetypal potentials are developed and expressed. This however, can also go the other way, external circumstances may in fact deny or suppress the expression of our archetypes.

To put all this in a practical context, let's say you want to create a meaningful career, but despite changing jobs a few times, you still end up with an unsatisfying job, or encounter similar problems in the new workplace. Or in a relationship context, you may wonder why you are often challenged by the same kinds of situations, or attracted to the same kind of men/women. You may have been consciously trying to do all the 'right' things, but those jobs or relationships just never work out quite the 'right' way for you. Instead of going outward, to find the best strategy or circumstance or person, it may be worth your while to go inward, to reflect on what your repetitive patterns are. Often you will find there is something you need to acknowledge and heal before you can move on from such a pattern. When you become aware and understand your archetypes, you become more conscious of the tendencies of your unconscious behavior, impulses, inclinations and triggers. More importantly, you become aware of how they relate to and affect your relationships with people in your life.

# Goddess Archetypes

Now we know that discovering our archetypes can help us to understand our unconscious way of thinking and our behavioural patterns. But there are many archetypes out there, so why do we use goddess archetypes?

I focus on mythical goddess archetypes in this book to understand our innate patterns for two main reasons. First, the goddess myths capture many aspects of the divine feminine power. The famed mythologist Joseph Campbell considered goddess *"the principle mythological role of the feminine principle: She gives birth to us physically, but She is the mother too of our second birth – our birth as spiritual entities"*[10]. The goddess is a mythological idea of a supernatural feminine figure. She symbolizes a great power that can bring out the truth and connect us to our spiritual centre, which can then lead us to conquer tremendous challenges and transform our lives for the better. The goddess is a psychological description of a complex female character that we can intuitively recognize both in ourselves and in the women around us.[11] Goddesses appear as superheroines in many myths. We admire these superheroines because we want to be like them, to succeed in pursuing our destiny. We want their courage, radiance and virtue, which are all part of our feminine potential.

Second, the mythical images of goddesses are deeply embedded in our collective unconscious across cultures and times. The images of goddesses in art, architecture and literature are everywhere. For example, the Temple of Athena Nike at the Acropolis in Athens is visited by millions of travellers each year. Renaissance masters such as Sandro Botticelli, Titian, Michelangelo, just to name a few, have all painted world famous paintings depicting goddesses. In the epic poems *Iliad* and *Odyssey* by Homer, the influence of goddesses is clearly significant. Even in today's popular culture, one of the latest blockbuster movies *Wonder Woman* features the goddess Diana (Artemis in Greek).

Therefore it is easy for us to relate to the goddess archetypes and what they symbolize and represent in women. We know them deeply in our collective psyche, which is the totality of our conscious and unconscious minds. There is a saying that feminine power has now awakened and risen, and from a social and political perspective, this is certainly correct. We can just look at the #MeToo movement, the Women's March, the increasing number of women working in upper management or as leaders in business and politics, even leading nations. However, from a spiritual perspective, feminine power has always been there with us, the difference is, we now have the opportunity to accept and embrace this power with more courage and conviction than ever before. Right now, women are speaking up and showing up. Some may even say we are living in the time of the Return of the Goddess.

## From Goddesses to Gods

So we can see how the concept of goddess archetypes helps us to understand our psyche, and how myths provide a perfect conduit for our unconscious mind to express into conscious awareness. Now let's look at the myths of the goddesses and how the feminine image has evolved through time.

The images of goddesses have lived among us throughout history. As early as the Paleolithic era, from 25,000 B.C. or earlier, painted caves and carved stone figures depicted goddesses[12]. These sculptures are often naked, voluptuous and pregnant to symbolize fertility and the power to bestow life. Probably the earlier and the most well-known goddess sculpture is the Venus of Willendorf, a small 11.1 centimetre tall figure found in 1908 at a paleolithic archaeological site in Austria. It is estimated that this Venus figurine was made between about 28,000 and 25,000 BCE.

As nature gave women the power to gestate and nourish, which in itself is a manifestation of the mystery of nature, it is not surprising to find images of goddesses being worshiped in the very early human world. Civilizations that worshipped goddesses were mostly agricultural tribes for example in Mesopotamia and Southeast Asia, but by the end of first millennium B.C, warrior tribes from Indo-European tribes had either taken over or merged with the planters[13]. The warriors brought male deities with them, and their gods married the local goddesses. In time, the cultures began to unify, and so their myths joined together as well.

Through thousands of years of human evolution, males have been biologically and psychologically wired to protect and support females, while females have the ability to give birth and nourish children. In many myths, we find an archetypical competitive nature among gods, which is contrasted with a cooperative nature among goddesses. At the time of the Trojan wars (around 1200 B.C.), patriarchal society rose in Greece, and Greek mythology from that time reflected this male-oriented warrior culture.

The myth about how Zeus became the most powerful god in the universe is a classical example. In classical Greek mythology, Gaia had long been considered the Mother of Earth. For a long time, there was only Gaia. She was the great goddess who provided nourishment for all forms of life. Later one of her sons, Uranus, who represents the sky, entered the myths and together they have many children, including the Titans and the Cyclopes.

Uranus was afraid to lose his power and authority to his children. In sharp contrast to Gaia's method of governing the earth, he forces them into a dark place deep beneath the surface of the earth. As a mother, Gaia became very upset with how her children were banished. She asked her children to stop Uranus. One of her sons, Cronus, came to her aid. Cronus defeated and castrated his own father, Uranus, and he threw Uranus's genitals into the sea. Interestingly, the reproductive part of Uranus merged with the sea foam and created Aphrodite, as a result of a fight for masculine power. She was nurtured by the feminine power, as the sea represents the regenerative power of mother nature, while Uranus's genitals, are the symbol of male power. This goddess has enormous transformative power and no man or god could force her to submit.

However, the myth does not stop here. As Cronus replaced his father, history repeated itself. Once again, Cronus's own son, Zeus, overthrew the Titans and took their place ruling the universe after he defeated of Cronus. Zeus, for fear of having the same destiny as his father and grandfather, ultimately sacrifices the goddess Metis, mother of his own daughter, Athena. As myths reflect social tension and dynamics, this myth shows us the competitive, ruthless and patriarchal culture of ancient Greece.

# Wisdom of the Myths

The more I dive into the world of myths, the more I see how mythology is grounded in social psychology and finds its peak in spirituality. As myths are the projection of our collective psyche, they reflect common fears, hopes, desires and conflicts experienced by people of their time. Through mythology we understand our social order, shared moral values, our human nature and our core spiritual beliefs. So, when myths are properly understood, they resonate with a personified energy dwelling within each individual, which can be conscious or unconscious. This is what happens when a particular myth spikes our interest or touches a chord, it is likely that an element of fear or desire has surfaced in our consciousness which we need to liberate and understand in order to grow.

Myths reflect the need for change on a personal level or the need for social and political revolution on a collective level, and they come with embedded ways to resolve the situations. The resolution or resurrection, however, tends to begin with an internal transformation. Even if the myth is about reaching a destination or winning a war, the ultimate victory lies in whether or not the Hero/Heroine has grown, and become the person he/she needs to be spiritually, in order to reach that final outcome.

Additionally, myths tell us that death is not the end of it all, our soul continues to live on and transcend our physical limitations. They helps us to shift our perception from body identification to spirit identification. Through mythology, we hold an image of the mystery of the universe and maintain a sense of awe of transcendence. We know our physical body is finite but our spirit self is infinite.

Interestingly, myths across different cultures and geographies have similar themes. For instance, one of the most common theme is crucifixion and resurrection.

We find that theme in the account of Jesus of Nazareth or in the myth of Osiris and Isis from Egypt. These are essentially death and rebirth scenarios. Some schools of thought suggest the similarities in mythical themes are due to the spread of culture through migration, while others believe these themes carry intrinsic elements of our collective psyche that tend to emerge through life.

We certainly do not read myths like we do historical records or scientific papers. What is important is that we look at the subtle meaning and moral lessons within the myths as they offer us insights on human nature, social dynamics and mystical wisdom.

So now let's begin with the myths of Athena, the goddess of wisdom and craft; and the archetype of The Strategist.

# Athena

## *Goddess of Wisdom and Craft*

Archetype: Strategist

*Palla Athena I begin to sing,*
*guardian of the city, the formidable goddess.*
*With Ares she cares for the work of war*
*the destruction of cities and the shouts of battle.*
*It is she who watches over the people,*
*When they go out to war and when they come back,*
*Farewell, goddess,*
*grant me good fortune and happiness too.*
**– HYMN TO ATHENA, The Homeric Hymns XI**[14]

## Who is Athena?

The archetype of Athena is active in a woman if she always has a mind, heart and spirit of her own. No matter whether it is about getting a research paper or business proposal in order, organizing a fundraiser, running a political campaign, relocating the entire family, or renovating a home, she can get everything done efficiently. She is independent and tends to be career or purpose-driven. The goddess archetype of Athena has a strong outward focus, to achieve goals and actualize her dreams. Athena usually makes her way through institutions, such as those found in education, culture, military, politics and business. She thrives in the city and holds her place well in the patriarchal culture.

The feminine power from Athena emerges from her intellect, determination and endurance, partly due to her ability to see the bigger picture. She can pull through difficult times because she has faith in herself, and she doesn't give up easily. She says, *"when there's a will, there's a way"*. In fact, more than just finding *a* way, she will find the *best* way.

As an archetype, Athena is smart, focused, pragmatic, yet highly creative. In war myths, she is often the strategist. She was known as the inventor of the bridle and the chariot for the horse, and she helped to construct the famous Wooden Horse that defeated Troy. Although in myths Poseidon ruled the seas and waves, Athena constructed the ship that could ride them. In contrast to Ares, the god of war, who represents indiscriminate rage and savagery, Athena employs skill and tactics, and in fact defeated Ares during the Trojan war.

Athena can always find the best way to get things done. Apart from being known as the goddess of wisdom, she is also a goddess of craft. She is a well-known weaver and excels at making aesthetic and functional items. However, she is not so keen on abstract or decorative art without any practical purpose.

So what makes Athena unique? What qualities differentiate her from other goddesses? Her myths offer us a clear picture of why she is who she is. We will start with the way how she came into the world.

## THE BIRTH OF ATHENA

The birth of Athena is a classical myth and a great example of the patriarchal culture assimilating the goddess. Zeus is an archetype that thrives on power and control. This does not come as a surprise given he has a family history of sons overthrowing their fathers. After years of pursuing her, Zeus finally wooed the wise titan goddess Metis and she became pregnant with his child.

An oracle told Zeus that Metis would have two children: the first would be wise and powerful, but the second one would kill him and take his throne. Zeus was alarmed by this omen and feared that history would repeat itself since he had killed his own father. He lured Metis close to him and when she was not paying attention, he swallowed her to eliminate her and the threat.

Some time later Zeus had an unbearable headache. He had Hephaestus, the god of metal and stone masonry, split open his head with an axe. At that instant, Athena sprang forth from Zeus's head, fully armed with a sharp spear. She looked majestic and regal. She gave a thunder-like loud cry that made all Olympus tremble. And that is how a powerful goddess such as Athena enters the world.

Despite her unusual birth, Athena is the favorite child of Zeus. He entrusted no other child, son or daughter, with the thunderbolt and the aegis, his symbols of power, only Athena.

# Archetype of a Strategist

The myths of Athena and her genealogy help us to understand her archetype. Athena was the right-hand person of Zeus because of her ability to carry power and use it wisely and diplomatically. As an archetype, Athena has patience and she negotiates strategically with the big picture in mind. She never acts on impulse or makes emotional decisions. She enjoys getting the approval and acknowledgment of her father. She is the ultimate 'father's daughter'. Fathers of Athenas are always very proud of their daughters and often boast that their daughters are just like them. Zeus is very impressed by Athena, and it is not hard to see why.

The myths tell of a great contest between Athena and Poseidon, the god of the seas. Both wanted to become the patron deity for the city state of Ancient Greece, and to decide the question they were both asked to offer a gift of true value for the city. Poseidon demonstrated his power by striking the earth with this trident, creating a well. It was a visually dramatic and impressive act and water started to flow immediately. However, the water was salty and so not particularly useful for the people. Next, it was Athena's turn. She simply stepped forward, pushed her spear into the ground and planted an olive branch in the hole. With that, olive trees started to grow and they brought olives and olive oil. These were incredibly useful gifts for the people, and the olive branch became a symbol of peace and prosperity. With the ability to see what is truly important, Athena won the contest and the city state of Athens was named after her.

Athena has many strengths, but she is not a natural mother. Instead she is more of a counsellor of male heroes. However she is in a sense the mother to Athens and the patron of civilized life. She is protectress of the city when it engages in war.

Athena watches over those who go to war, and their return. The passage in the *Hymn to Athena* quoted at the start of this chapter reminded me of how England's Queen Elizabeth I rode her horse to directly address her troops at Tilbury in preparation for repelling the expected invasion by the Spanish Armada in 1588. Like Athena, Elizabeth was never married and she was also known as a patient and effective strategist.

Later we will examine stories where goddesses are seduced, kidnapped and exploited. Only a few escape this treatment, such as Athena and Artemis, known as the virgin goddesses. These two goddesses are independent of domination by gods or free from romantic entanglement.

## Patrons of the heros

The Athena archetype is driven by the goals of accomplishment and victory. She is a powerful ally and advisor. In her myths, Athena inspires and supports the heroes. For example when Odysseus was trying to make his way home after ten years battling the Trojan War, Athena helped him and his son Telemachus to avoid danger and overcome great difficulties. She offered them insight and caution. The hero eventually reunited with his wife Penelope in Ithaca after another ten-year journey home. Athena helped both the father and son because she respected their courage and determination to unite the family after nearly twenty years. She appears to those in desperate need of her help as she is compassionate and kind, but she only helps those who are fair and deserving of her help.

Athena is the goddess who can keep her poise no matter what is happening, and she bides her time, acting only when the timing is right. Athena thinks rationally and strategically. In the *Iliad*, she came to Achilles when he needed self-discipline and prevented him from drawing his sword in his quarrel with king Agamemnon. She also shape-shifted to help him kill Hector, the prince of Troy, causing a dramatic pivot in the war. Although it was an unfortunate outcome for the Trojans, it was the beginning of the end of a very long war between the two nations.

The qualities of impulse control and restraint are Athena's strengths, and the intelligence to see beyond immediate gratification is her gift. She offers good counsel, with practical foresight, and urges her heroes to think things through, specially at critical moments. She represents practical wisdom and strategic counsel.

The Athena archetype within us embodies the feminine power that creates women who are inspiring, wise and admirable. Her qualities are found in excellent mentors, coaches, consultants, advisors, supportive roles and leaders in any profession or academia.

In many classical paintings, we see Athena dressed in full armour, looking beautiful and stately. She is often depicted with an owl with prominent eyes which symbolizes wisdom and knowledge. On her shield or breastplate, we often see the image of Medusa's head as a reminder of the myth of Perseus. When Perseus was tricked and forced to slay the Gorgon Medusa in order to save himself and his mother, Athena gave him a shining bronze shield. Using this as a mirror, he could see Medusa, without actually meeting her eye and the lethal gaze that turned humans into stone. With Athena's help, Perseus succeeded in beheading Medusa and eventually he gave the head to Athena in tribute. Symbolically, the true gift from Athena is the ability to reflect. Medusa, the scary-looking monster with snakes as her hair, represents fear. The way to face and master fear is to look within, to engage in reflection before action. That is the wisdom of Athena.

Athena's myths often emphasis the value of strategic thinking, she looks at the optimal outcomes before carefully considering the appropriate immediate response.

All these Athena's myths give us similar clues about the archetype she represents. You may wonder if you or someone close to you embodies an active Athena archetype. So next, we will turn to a modern-day context and look deeper into the relationships of contemporary Athenas.

# ATHENA DAUGHTER AND MOTHER

A young Athena seems to be a grown-up child and has a mind of her own. She spends lots of time thinking, understanding and rationalizing things. The most natural thing for an Athena to do is to focus on her studies and stay away from family tensions. She likes to spend time on her interests and never makes a fuss unless she needs to defend what she wants to do.

An Athena daughter doesn't give her parents much boy trouble, as opposed to an Aphrodite daughter who may cause her mother concern about the sort of boys she attracts, or a Hera who soon starts dreaming about marriage or a Demeter who may want to have a baby early.

As Athena grows up, she becomes increasingly independent and likes to make decisions for herself. If Athena has a Persephone mother, the archetype of an eternal maiden, an Athena may be "mothering" her own mother and trying to organize family matters in her mother's stead. If she has an Artemis mother, who prefers the wilderness to the city, mother and daughter are likely to have very different preferences, tastes and orientations in their lifestyle choices. However, both are strong and independent women in the family, and likely to be busy with their own pursuits.

Some life circumstances can make a young girl become more of an Athena even though it isn't the most natural archetype active in her. If her parents are physically or emotionally unavailable, or if the family is in any kind of hardship, a daughter will have to step up and help her siblings or even support her family. It is not only nature, but external situations that can influence the archetypes active in us.

If Athena is the mother, she will be highly efficient and organised. She will make sure the house in order, that her daughter is well provided for her material needs. She will research and read widely on pregnancy, childbirth and developmental milestones for her child. An Athena mother will also place a high priority on the education of her child.

For an Athena to have a child, it also signals that she has reached a new stage in her life. She may still be very focused on her career but she wants more than just work in life. She is aware of the energy required to raise a child, but she is also willing to give and receive more love in her life. It can be a challenging transition because she needs to shift her focus from her own external goals to her child's wellbeing. Though she may understand intellectually the extent of the effort and energy it takes to raise a child, the actual experience will be different. Needless to say, this transition brings maturity and growth, particularly for an Athena. It will balance her life from one asking *"What do I want to achieve?"* to one asking *"How may I serve?"*.

The chances are, by the time an Athena wants to have a family, the energy of Demeter has started to have an influence on her. Demeter is the nurturer and mother archetype which we will consider in chapter five. Sometimes an Athena will never have any biological children, but she may want to mentor or teach, to give more of herself to others. She may like to share her success and wisdom when she reaches a certain stage of maturity in her life.

## THE CAREER WOMAN

After examining Athena's myths, it is not hard to picture her as the career woman or scholar among us. Her greatest asset is her intellectual mind and ability to focus. With these attributes, Athena can succeed in any field of her choosing.

She may work her way up in a corporation or institution and eventually become part of the management or the CEO of the company. She may be the right-hand person of the CEO or heir to a business empire for a long time, so she can learn how to run the business before eventually taking over. Athena can also be an entrepreneur, academic, scientist or medical professional.

She is a high achiever in any organization. She can also be highly successful in politics because of her can-do attitude and strategic thinking. Her only issue is building warm and loyal relationships with voters or the colleagues around her. People admire her hard-working ethics and determination to make progress, but this is a double-edged sword, as people may fear she will do anything necessary to achieve her goals. Athena's biggest challenge is to build trust, to assure people that she will do the right thing even if it causes setbacks.

A more mature Athena will likely to shift her focus from her self-interest to the interests of others, as in the case of being a mother or a mentor. After years of accomplishments, she may come to a stage in life where she begins to question what she really wants or needs.

The ability to reflect is also part of Athena's gift. A younger Athena will tend to reflect on how to improve her work or circumstances, but later on, self-reflection will lead her towards the things in her life that really matter. There is no distance between our head and heart, but sometimes it can take a long time for an Athena to get there.

We can of course have more than one archetype active in us. If a woman has both Artemis and Athena in her, she will be highly effective in achieving her noble cause, or anything that she is passionate about. Oprah Winfrey is a good example. She is a powerful woman in the entertainment business and at the same time she is well known for her philanthropy efforts in educating young girls and empowering women. She is an advocate for meditation and is renowned for her love of gardening, being in nature and her dogs. These qualities further solidify her image as a hybrid goddess who holds many of the attributes of both Athena and Artemis. If a woman is a hybrid between Athena and Hera, she is likely to be the wife of a successful man, though she is also known for her own abilities. The US first lady Eleanor Roosevelt is a notable example. She was highly respected and admired and made many public appearances on behalf of her husband President Franklin Roosevelt. She continued to be an activist, advocating for the expansion of women's roles in the workplace and civil rights, for 17 years after the death of her husband.

## Relationships with Athena

Although Athena is never married in her myths, women who have Athena as a dominant archetype have romantic relationships and marriages just like other archetypes. However, it is unlikely for an Athena to fall head over heels in love easily or frequently. Especially for a young and ambitious Athena, who wants to focus on her studies or work, romance may simply becomes a distraction. But that isn't to say she won't fall in love and have a family. She may do so, just never in a rush or carelessly. Athena is responsible and likes to plan ahead. She tends to be attracted to powerful and successful men who stand out in their own right. She is drawn to men she admires or respects greatly.

If a relationship blossoms, marriage is certainly an option for Athena. She will be very rational in terms of how to go about the wedding and when to start a family. If her marriage does not last and results in a divorce, she is unlikely to have an emotional outburst, but rather carefully consider her options and how to process the change of circumstance. She may even remain friends with her ex-husband if the break up is amicable.

Sometimes Athena may come across as cold or aloof to those who care about her. Her family and friends may feel she keeps a distance. In reality, it may not necessarily be the case. It is true that she is more rational than emotional, and she will choose thinking over feeling, but that is just her psychological type. It is not that she is incapable of loving, she certainly does, but it is her expression of love that differs from others. Also people who are not familiar with her archetype may have expectations of her that may lead to inaccurate impressions.

An Athena will probably prefer helping her siblings with homework than spending time playing with them. She may offer financial support to her family more readily than time commitment. If a tragedy strikes her family, she will be the one who takes charge as she feels she is responsible for leading everyone through.

Of course Athena has her emotional life too, but she can always keep her head above water and see the bigger picture. She tends to manage, if not control, her emotions. In her myths, she always appears to her heroes at the most critical times, when they are about to commit a mistake because they are overwhelmed by fear or anger. Athena always knows the right thing to do, even if it is not an easy or comfortable thing to do. With relationships, sometimes the right thing to do is to say no, and say it with love. For example, if a child wants to touch a fire, it is a loving thing to say no to her. By the same token, if Athena sees a loved one is in a situation that will cause them harm, her loving response will be to block the situation. Athena has the ability to observe, reflect and then respond appropriately. It is not because she is cold, but because she is calm. Athena is an incredible, wise and loyal ally, and she delivers on her promises.

## What can we learn from Athena?

If you are planning to begin a new course of study, change your career, start a new business or take on a big change in life, Athena is a great goddess to call upon or look to as a role model. Not only is she wise, determined and able to find the best way to get things done, she possesses a great ability to see the big picture, control impulses and make rational decisions. She is a great ally no matter what natural active archetypes you may have.

If you have Hera, the goddess of marriage naturally active in you, by inviting the attributes of Athena into your life, you will gain a stronger sense of self-worth and feel empowered to pursue other interests or purposeful projects beside your marriage. If as a Hera you unfortunately have to go through a divorce, the Athena archetype will help you to heal, grow and move on to a new chapter in life.

If Athena is an archetype active in your mother or in you, while other women around you have different archetypes, you may begin to think about the differences in communication styles that come from this archetype. Athena does not express her love and care in the same way as other archetypes, she may give advice or provide help in a practical manner instead of warmer or more comforting gestures. However, she can be extremely supportive, loyal and true to her word.

By having a better understanding and realistic expectations of your own and others' archetypes, you can improve your relationships with people around you.

## WAYS TO GROW BEYOND

Just like a coin, there are two sides to Athena. The nature of duality, Yin and Yang, exist in all things. When Athena is out of balance, she may overthink and over analyse situations. Athena's mind is her strongest asset, and she has a tendency to stay in her head and disconnect from her heart.

Being rational and pragmatic may have an advantage in work, study, or facing challenges, but with relationships it may not always be the case. We know externally she will respond well, but she needs to be mindful about how she is processing her emotions internally, if she processes them at all. She may function very well by staying in an emotional vacuum, but over time, she may lose her ability to connect with her own emotions, or know what her heart truly desires.

Another tendency of Athena is to be disconnected from her body. No one can rationalize the intimacy of a relationship, or be pragmatic about the sensuality of a woman. This is for a woman to experience, not to accomplish.

An Athena who is evolving into a more mature and spiritually conscious woman will start to feel new emotions being stirred in her heart. At a certain point, with all the worldly accomplishments she has accumulated, she may question, *"is there all there is?"*. What will now satisfy or fulfill her begins to change. She may actually feel a little uneasy with this new sense of desire, and the need to feel inspired. This may lead to a new passion or pursuit of a more meaningful life. She may like to express her creativity more than ever before. It is also likely that she will feel the influence of other goddesses start to activate at this time. If it is Hera, the desire to get married and be in partnership will start to grow in her. If it is Demeter, the idea of having a family with children to nurture will become appealing.

Several years ago I came to know an Athena woman called Betty. She had gone through a typical Athena journey. Betty held an upper management position in a financial corporation. For years her focus was her career and she travelled the world for her work. She and her husband lived in their dream house and enjoyed luxurious vacations every year. However, financial abundance and a comfortable lifestyle are only part of the story.

As her accomplishments and maturity grew, the sense of something missing also became more apparent. She felt empty inside, no beautiful furniture or clothes or material objects could fill the void. Her health also suffered due to long working hours, travel, stress and hostile professional environments. She became increasingly interested in spirituality, energy healing and astrology. She immersed herself in studying a wide variety of metaphysical subjects and she found them deeply fulfilling for her soul. She knew she had outgrown her previous self. Eventually she left her corporate job and created a successful purpose-driven, spiritually based business. The transition was not without challenges, she had to let go of material things and open up a space for new experiences to come in. Within a few short years she made her transition. She became a leader and influencer in her industry, which is not surprising with her Athena qualities. Her Athena archetype never left her as she explored her spiritual side, she remained a very wise business woman, but she evolved and blossomed.

We are all spirit having a human experience. For an Athena to grow, she will need to learn how to let go and follow the lead of the universe. This may not be an easy task for her, as this concept is non-rational, but not irrational. There is a power greater than ourselves. Some may call it God or the creator, or the universe or source, whichever language you prefer, there is a divine intelligence that programs a bud to become a rose, an embryo to become a baby. It is not irrational to follow this intelligence and allow our life to unfold in a similar way.

It is important for an Athena to take cues from life and to be aware when it is time to move and when it is time to stay still. It may feel uneasy at first because it may feel like giving up control, but in fact it is not. There are certain things in life we can change, but there are things that we cannot, like our family or race, and the wisdom lies in knowing the difference.

An Athena needs to get over the motto that *"I want to get what I want, and I am going to make it happen"*. It requires a higher level of consciousness and intelligence to know that sometimes a self-initiated plan can be a good plan, but it is not necessarily the right plan. We need to do our part, to speak up or show up in life when we feel it is the right thing to do and we are inspired to act in a certain way. But to forcefully push forward with our own agenda without going inward or knowing if it is a higher calling, is not strategic or wise.

As Athena comes to an older age, she may find herself uncomfortable with the idea of depending on other people. She is an archetype that is very independent from an early age and doesn't like to be vulnerable or dependent. In fact, allowing ourselves to feel vulnerable is often like stepping on the edge of enlightenment. It is in that vulnerability that we open our hearts, to be more compassionate and kind to ourselves and others. It is a natural progress for Athena to move more towards the sense of receptivity, to slow down and start to live in the feeling of gratitude more. To do that, very often the first step is to allow others to help and to connect. When that happens, Athena will inevitably find a deeper sense of peace and fulfillment which external goals were never able to provide. This is an inner experience that perhaps she was always missing but never realised.

Growth may feel uncomfortable at first, as it stretches us further than we are used to being. Just like when we were children, growing taller may give us some aches. But all these changes are helping an Athena to become more balanced and whole, instead of one-sided and externally focused. It will help her not just in reaching higher, but also in living a deeper life.

# Self-care for Athena

## Aromatherapy

As Athena is someone who is intellectual, focused, rational, sharp and often uses her head instead of listening to her heart, her blend should include herbaceous essentials such as rosemary, basil and peppermint blended together with fresh, sharp-scented citrus oils such as lemon or lime. A dash of ginger would also be perfect! This should all be balanced with a wood oil such as sandalwood.

*For more information on Aromatherapy and the Goddesses, please refer to Appendix 1.*

## Wellness practices

Exercises that can help to connect body and mind will be beneficial for an Athena. Spending time in nature will also help to strengthen the connection with the environment outside of her mind.

- Yoga, dancing
- Bushwalking, outdoor exercise, swimming in the ocean

- Meditation – this is a very important one, whichever style or form undertaken, the benefits of meditation will be tremendous for this archetype.
- Engage in a creative project such as pottery, ceramics or knitting.
- Work with a coach to open up a dialogue for personal growth

##  Note-to-self

*"The end is inherent in the means."*
– Mahatma Gandhi

*"Happiness is not a goal; it is a by-product."*
– Eleanor Roosevelt

## Self-reflective questions

You may like to answer these self-reflective questions as you read through this book or schedule some quiet time in your week to focus on going within. It may be a nice way to prepare yourself by doing a 10 to 15-minute meditation before writing down your thoughts. There are no rules; whichever ways can help you to connect with your inner self will be beneficial to you.

- Do you tend to make decisions based on thinking, rather than feeling?
- Are you often valued as an analytical person and called a problem-solver?
- Do you follow your inner guidance?

- Do you value intuition and mystical or transcendent experiences? Did you use to?
- What qualities of Athena can you see in yourself?
- Do you recognize Athena as a natural archetype that is active in you, or is she sometimes activated due to external circumstances? If so, what are they?
- If Athena is a minor archetype active in you, an ally to provide more strength to other archetypes, who is your more dominant archetype? (Hera/wife, Demeter/mother, Artemis/activist or Aphrodite/lover, transformer) You may like to come back to this question later after reading more on other goddess archetypes.
- Do you have Athena/s in your life? Are they members of your family, perhaps your sister, or mother? Maybe your friend or acquaintance? Colleague or boss? How do you get along with her?
- If Athena is not active in you, what part of her qualities or strengths would you like to develop?

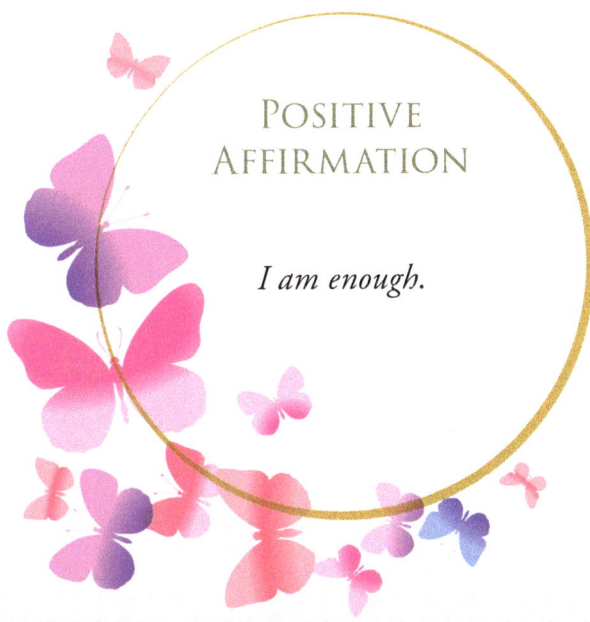

## Positive Affirmation

*I am enough.*

# Artemis

## *Goddess of Moon and Hunt*

Archetype: Activist, Protector

*Every part of this earth is sacred to my people.
Every shining pine needle, every sandy shore, every mist in the dark woods,
every meadow, every humming insect.
All are holy in the memory and experience of my people.
We know the sap which courses through the trees
as we know the blood that courses through our veins.
We are part of the earth and it is part of us.*
– **Chief Seattle, 1855**[15]

# WHO IS ARTEMIS?

I have no doubt that any Artemis who reads the entirety of Chief Seattle's letter will be moved and deeply resonate with his sentiment about our sacred earth. The Greek goddess Artemis (Diana in Roman) is known as the Huntress and Goddess of the Moon. She is the protector of nature, justice and women. As a fierce archer, Artemis never misses her target. Similar to Athena, she can focus on her goals and inspirations, but Artemis thrives in the wilderness while Athena rules the city.

Homer's 'Hymn to Artemis'[16], depicts this beautiful goddess's delight in chasing her prey deep into the dark forests and high mountains. She launches her golden arrows and we hear the howling sound of wild animals. At night, with her heart elated, she goes to dance with the Muses and Graces. As a moon goddess, Artemis is associated with winter solstice, and she connects us with our feminine mysteries and intuition. The reflective nature of moon illuminates us during the dark nights of our soul, and it reminds us that we are never truly alone, even if we are in solitude. On a physical level, we appear as separate human beings, but from a spiritual perspective, all of our consciousness is joined. We are all spirit having a human experience. We are one and eternally connected.

There are times an Artemis craves her own time with nature to simply connect with her inner self. She needs time to recharge and to reflect. It may be camping in the woods, walking in the park or simply sitting outdoors under the stars.

In classical paintings, we often see Artemis wearing a crown-shaped crescent moon upon her brow, which can also symbolize animal horns. She often holds a bow and arrow, and is accompanied by animals such as a stag or bear in lush forest surrounds.

Apart from her connection with nature, Artemis also gravitates towards sisterhood and is a protector of women, children and the weak in need of help. Straight after the goddess Leto gave birth to Artemis, she helped her mother as a midwife to safely deliver Apollo, her twin brother. Therefore, she is known as heaven's midwife who keeps pregnant women safe and helps to smooth labour and delivery.

In mythology, Artemis chooses her own companions and many of them are woodland nymphs. She defends their virginity as well as protecting them from peeping hunters. Artemis never marries and has no children in her myths, but sometimes she is pictured as a mother bear, fiercely defending those she loves. By extension, she is also the guardian of forests and wild spaces of the world. Artemis is often invoked when protection is sought for women or the planet Earth.

# Archetype of a Protector and Activist

Artemis is a passionate warrior in many ways. When she finds a cause that is worth fighting for, she will immerse herself fully in the mission. Since she is naturally drawn to the calling of preserving nature and helping women, two women come to my mind who deeply connect with the image of Artemis. One is Dame Jane Morris Goodall, the world-renowned expert on chimpanzees, she has worked extensively on conservation and animal welfare issues for over 50 years. The other is Ruth Bader Ginsberg, an Associate Justice of the Supreme Court of the United States. For over 40 years, she has been publicly advocating gender equality and women's rights as a woman, wife and mother. Ginsberg experienced discrimination as a law student and in her early career but she rose as a modern icon of a powerful woman who persevered and succeeded. Both modern Artemis women have been on their path of truth for decades. They have stood firm and tall on what they believe and invested a tremendous effort in creating real change for the better.

Artemis women do not give up easily. They have strong wills, and they believe in fairness and justice. They have incredible energy to sustain their lifelong passions for their cause/s. Many Artemis women have Athena as an ally in their psyche. It is not surprising as, in order to succeed in their causes, they often need to develop some of Athena's attributes such as patience, great intellectual capacity and pragmatism in their pursuits.

When an Artemis needs time off, she will always prefer to connect with nature, as the majestic power of nature will soothe her and bring her clarity. She may hear a calling for creativity or procreation in her later years, and this is often a call to invite other goddesses in to further her growth.

## Artemis in action

Since Artemis is purpose-driven, with great determination, energy and perseverance, she often has many accomplishments. She enjoys competition and she receives plenty of recognition because of her many achievements. However, she is not motivated by an ego-driven agenda or fame. She simply wants to do her best in the things that she is interested in or to succeed in her goals. When an Artemis woman faces an obstacle, it will not deter her sense of direction, but only lead her to rise higher to overcome the challenge. In her myths, she is a highly competitive archer and hunter.

Many Artemis women are professional athletes or love to play sports as a hobby. They enjoy the intensity and excitement of competitions. It energizes them and makes them feel alive. Since Artemis loves the outdoors, women who have Artemis has a dominant archetype may choose to work outdoors, or has a strong aspect of physical mobility or prefers proximity to nature. Professions that are related to environmental conservation, animal welfare, botany, earth sciences or astronomy can also be very appealing for an Artemis.

Artemis cares deeply about women, children and those who are in adversity and need protection. She may be drawn to become a gynecologist, midwife or pediatrician. It is not hard to find an Artemis joining or leading a women's movement or efforts for social change. We may see her working or volunteering in women's shelters, helping sexually or physically abused women in a clinic or teaching self-protection classes.

Artemis represents independent thinking and someone who is not easily influenced by other people's opinions. She doesn't need a man's approval or the Miss Popular vote. She speaks her truth and listens to her heart.

If an Artemis chooses to enter a helping profession, or a legal field or politics, she usually has an ideal that influences her voice. She may feel strongly about the need to bring change to some current social issue or injustice. She will be the frontrunner to stand up or speak up, while an Athena may be the person who provides strategy in the background. If Artemis is in a creative or inspirational field, all her work will also reflect a personal vision, there is always meaning and purpose in her work. If an Artemis is in business, she must believe in its value or impact.

A mature Artemis often finds herself interested in spiritual or mystic matters that bring up a higher level of consciousness. She may or may not change her career in response, but there is a growing undercurrent in her work that connects to the deeper meaning in life, and what truly matters to her heart. As a moon goddess, it is not surprising that an Artemis woman feels increasing drawn to moon energy, its reflective nature and the power of feminine energy.

## Myths of Artemis

Artemis' mother Leto was a Titan, one of the divinities that used to rule the earth before Zeus and his fellow Olympians took over. You can imagine a little Artemis, having an independent mind of her own, curious about the world and wanting to explore everything around her. Her eyes would be full of wonder and the spark of intrigue. She would be totally absorbed by the things that interest her and fast to protest if her adventures were disrupted. She would not tolerate dishonesty or unfair treatment to anyone or anything. Now Artemis, being the daughter of Zeus and Leto, was only finally introduced to her father at the age of three. Even at their first meeting, Zeus was very taken by her. He was charmed by her character and how different she was compared to other young goddesses. He asked her, if she could have any gift from him, what would her heart desire? Her answers were indeed different from most girls her age. She wanted a silver bow, arrows and dogs to hunt with in the vast forest. She also wanted to wear a short tunic so that she could run faster in the woods. She desired to have sister playmates but only if she could choose them. Not only did Zeus fulfil all of her unusual requests, he has also became incredibly fond of her.

With her tools and abilities, Artemis can be very effective in the world. She can aim for her targets and achieve them. Her silver bow and arrow also have a connection with the moon energy, a feminine quality that represents inner self-reflection and mystical awareness.

As a goddess of the wilderness, her realm is full of wild animals. The animal most prevalent in her mythology is the mother bear, which symbolizes Artemis herself, and there are also plenty of stags, deers and hounds. Her companions, the nymphs, are minor divinities of the forest, lakes, mountains and trees.

# The myth of Atalanta

Atalanta was a mortal woman who had many of the attributes of Artemis and was watched over by the goddess. Atalanta was heir to the king of Arcadia, but when she was born, the king became very angry that Atalanta was a girl, not a boy. He wanted a male heir, and so he sent his servants to abandon her in the mountains. However, Atalanta was blessed with the protection of Artemis, a mother bear smelled her sweet scent and was attracted by the noise she made. When the mother bear approached Atalanta, she grabbed onto the mother bear's fur and didn't let go. Atalanta and the mother bear formed a bond and so she was taken back to the bear den like a cub in the mountains.

As Atalanta was raised by the mother bear, the wilderness became her home. She was found by some hunters later on who then taught her language and how to use a bow and arrow. They were delighted by this little girl who excelled in everything they could teach her. As Atalanta matured into her womanhood, she joined a famous hunter called Meleager for the Calydonian Boar Hunt. At first many hunters were angry that a woman was joining the hunt, but then several of the men were killed by the boar and Meleager convinced them to let Atalanta join the hunt. Eventually it was Atalanta who wounded the boar with her arrows, enabling Meleager to seize the defining moment and kill the boar with his spear. With this victory, Atalanta became a famous huntress. Eventually the king of Arcadia heard her story and realised she was his abandoned heir. At the end, father and daughter reconciled their relationship and Atalanta's royal birthright was restored.

As discussed in chapter one, the wisdom of mythology can tell us a lot about the social values and moral codes at the time of the myth. The importance of having a male heir is a significant one in many cultures. Even in recent years in China, when the one-child policy (1979–2016) was in effect, many families would go to great lengths to try to conceive a boy. This preference has created imbalance in the collective psyche, as if boys are somehow more important and valued than girls. The myth of Atalanta shows this issue in the extreme, but it brings out moral lesson to a social issue. Think about the hurt inflicted in the psyche of a young girl who is told that her father would have preferred her to be a boy. Some girls would be motivated to be high achievers to prove their worth. For others, it would diminish their self-esteem and confidence from an early age. An Artemis will not submit to such prejudice. She will stand out and speak up for others if need be. She will prove her worth and significance.

# Artemis daughter and mother

As myths speak metaphorically, not factually, the myth of Atalanta can also represent a girl who appears to be a disappointment to her father and so is abandoned literally or emotionally. Perhaps it is the sense of not meeting the expectation of how a daughter is "supposed" to be in a particular family. For parents who dream of a quiet, compliant daughter who loves to play house with dolls, an Artemis daughter is unlikely to be appreciated or even accepted.

When a child expresses her natural archetype but it is not what her parents expected her to be, she will sometimes feel discouraged or even rejected. She may choose to hide that side of her natural self as she grows up in order to fit into the expectations of the family or, in a broader sense, what she perceives society asks of her. Our perception can be easily influenced during our formative years and she may not even be conscious about such a denial of her natural archetype. That said, there are strong Artemis girls that would rather be free than liked or accepted. Also when Artemis finds her purpose or cause, she will pursue it passionately, regardless of whether or not she receives the approval of others.

It is easy to spot a young Artemis daughter. She loves to be outdoors, especially in nature. Dress ups or playing house will not be her favourite games, she much prefers to play with animals or run free. She has a mind of her own, and she can spend hours exploring matters that interest her instead of longing for the attention of others. She may even seem distant because she is so absorbed in her own world of wonders and intrigues.

Some years ago I met an Artemis mother called Jane in one of my workshops. Jane was tall, fit and has a beautiful sun-kissed tan. She dressed like an earth goddess and advocated natural, organic skincare products. She was passionate in helping women to heal through nutrition and herbal medicine. Needless to say, she loved the great outdoors. At the workshop, I talked about the goddess archetypes. When I was describing Artemis, her face started to light up. After the workshop she told me that she knew Artemis was her natural archetype and she had always been a free spirit and true to herself. Now that she was a mother, although she loved her daughter unconditionally, there was a part of her that just wanted to spend time alone in nature. But she felt guilty to even want to do that.

It is only natural for an Artemis to want to recharge and restore her energy by immersing in nature alone. I explained to Jane that it is important to fulfill that need, to think of it like a detox or spring clean. It can bring much needed vitality into life. Jane could only be her best self (and best mum) if she fully embraced and accepted who she was deep inside. It is not an act of abandonment if she arranged care for her daughter, perhaps even made it a fun experience for her daughter to spend time with other members of the family or friends. For an Artemis, this is an act of ultimate self-care. Jane was relieved to hear that and was eager to plan a hiking day for herself and a special outing for her daughter.

When we fully accept who we are, we become empowered. Self-acceptance is essentially an act of love towards ourselves, and only when we can achieve that, can we truly accept others. You can't give away what you don't have. You only know how to truly love someone if you have experienced love yourself. You may not receive love from the same person you are giving it to, but you know how love feels if you have experienced it yourself.

## Relationships with Artemis

Although Artemis never marries in her myths, many Artemis women I have met are married or in relationships. One thing that is always true for an Artemis is that she needs space and independence. Just as she can dedicate herself to her passionate causes, she can commit to important relationships. But she does not appreciate being "boxed in" and it may take a little time for her to adjust at first. She needs her freedom to conduct her life and sometimes she needs her time off to retreat into nature or a weekend away, all alone. This is not a sign of her lack of interest or commitment to a relationship, but sometimes people around her may feel left behind or abandoned.

Learning about the archetype of Artemis helps anyone in a relationship with her to understand its dynamics. She may or may not reciprocate the shape or form of the relationship you have in mind, so clear communication with her will be important. Artemis women are very loyal and protective. They are honest and straightforward. They won't play manipulative games or take relationships lightly.

The myth of Actaeon shows the tragic consequences if you anger this powerful goddess. One day Artemis was bathing in the woods, accompanied by her companions. The hunter Actaeon stumbled across the naked goddess and her nymphs, and, motivated by lust and her ravishing beauty, he stopped and stared. When Artemis discovered him, she was furious. He had disgraced her as a goddess, but more than that he had disgraced her nymphs. Artemis had always been fiercely protective of the virginity of her nymphs, and she didn't want this story to encourage other hunters to lust after her nymphs. Artemis forbade Actaeon from speaking of the incident. However, when he heard his hunting party, he couldn't help but call out to them. At that instant, Artemis transformed him into a stag. When he realized what had happened, he fled into the woods. Unfortunately his own hounds caught up with him, and failed to recognize Actaeon as their master. The hounds tore him into pieces.

This tragic myth serves as an cautionary tale about Artemis. Firstly, she is very protective towards the people she cares about, and secondly, you don't get many chances with her. If you get on the wrong side of an Artemis, she will not let you get away with your wrongdoing very easily. One way or another, she will ensure justice is served.

## What can we learn from Artemis?

The greatest attribute of Artemis is her capacity to focus on something of her own choosing. Her dedication, authenticity and determination are qualities that we can all learn from. Her passionate pursuits are not bound by people's opinions and do not require anyone's approval. She has a heart and mind of her own. She is fiercely compassionate towards causes she believes in, especially those concerning the environment, wildlife, women and children. She seeks justice when there is any victimization or inequality. She doesn't fear or crave power but only wants to restore healthy checks and balances.

An Artemis does not stay in one place, she will always take actions to move forward, guided by her own conscience and beliefs. When you share a bond with an Artemis, she will offer you her lifelong loyalty, fair judgement, honest opinion and unbreakable integrity.

## Ways to grow beyond

Every archetype has major gifts, but in the extreme, or in their shadow aspects, they can make mistakes. The good news is you can always draw upon the strength of other archetypes, as human beings are adaptable and changeable. We can learn from our mistakes or other people's mistakes.

Artemis in the extreme can impose her sense of righteousness upon other people. When she sees wrongdoing or unfairness, she may become outraged and act impulsively. At times she may even damage the situation more than benefit it. She will need to learn how to be more patient and refrain from acting out of emotions. She may find it difficult to control her reactions, especially when she strongly believes she is right. She will need to learn that sometimes it is better not to act immediately or say things the way she wants to say them. It is important to be able to detach and reflect first, especially with matters close to heart. That's why Athena is a great goddess to have as an ally. She will be able to calm Artemis down and think strategically at the most heated moments.

Another tendency of Artemis is becoming too goal-focused and competitive. Since she cares deeply about her causes and principles, she may come across as uncompromising or even stubborn. She may be impatient to see how life may unfold when she is not actively pursuing goals or causes. She may struggle with the feeling of "not good enough" or keep chasing the next level of achievement endlessly.

Artemis is a powerful and willful goddess, so the challenge is not to be strong, but to be vulnerable. For some this may mean learning to love and care deeply about another person, through a relationship with a man or woman, or by having a child. Often an Artemis will go through a change when she matures and turns more inward. It is not always bound by age, as life experiences can make us more mature. As Artemis grows, she will learn to become more patient and go slower. She will go inward more deeply before making an important decision, and be less affected by the burning need to have certainty and control over things in life.

If the influence of Aphrodite is brought in through love of, or toward, another person, she will become aware that she has needs for intimacy as well as for independence, and the art is to learn how to balance the two. She can become more inner-directed as well as outer-focused.

If the influence of Demeter comes into her life, an Artemis will consider having a child, mentoring a protege, or become a custodian of a project.

When an Artemis is going through change, the key approach is to centre herself and make time to reflect. As a result, her competitiveness and impatience may ease and create more time and space to allow people to come into her life.

# Self-care for Artemis

## Aromatherapy

As Artemis prefers nature, has a strong spirit and tends to be an activist, her blend should include light florals such as rose otto or neroli, blended together with frankincense, rich piney-scented oils such as fir, pine or spruce. This would be beautifully balanced by cedarwood.

*For more information on Aromatherapy and the Goddesses, please refer to Appendix 1.*

## Wellbeing practices

Artemis will benefit greatly from time outdoors in nature. Whether it is to camp or hike in the wilderness, sit under the stars at night, spend time with animals or simply hug a tree, earthly connections will be soul-nourishing for an Artemis. Other physical activities she would enjoy include:

- Yoga – to calm the mind and benefit many other body systems
- Meditation – to practice stillness and to go inward

- Any sports – it is more than likely that an Artemis has been playing some form of competitive sports in her early years or all her life. The key is to keep her body moving!
- Gardening
- Horse riding

## ❝ Note-to-self:

*"True freedom is understanding that we have a choice in who and what we allow to have power over us."*
– Meryl Streep

*"Only actions originated from love can bring peace, anything else will only bring more of the same thing."*
– Anonymous

## Self-reflective questions

You may like to answer these self-reflective questions as you read through this book or schedule some quiet time in your week to focus on going within. It may be a nice way to prepare yourself by doing a 10 to 15-minute meditation before writing down your thoughts. There are no rules; whichever ways can help you to connect with your inner self will be beneficial to you.

- Artemis has quite a few different qualities, which ones do you align with?
- Which positive qualities would you like to develop the most?
- Is there someone you know that clearly has the qualities of an Artemis?

- ❧ Do you feel there is a need to balance your independence and intimacy?
- ❧ Are you aware of your passion and purpose?
- ❧ Are you in tune with what you really want to do or experience in life?
- ❧ Are there any dreams that you have been unable or unwilling to pursue in the past?
- ❧ Can you see the goodness in all your relationships, even if they didn't last or work out the way you intended?
- ❧ Do you allow yourself to feel your emotions and know that it is your natural guiding system?
- ❧ Are you able to see how your life unfolds with synchronicity, knowing all things are meant to happen in a certain way to bring you to where you are today?
- ❧ What would be most soul satisfying for you now? What is it that you deeply desire?
- ❧ What makes you feel the most meaning and fulfilment at this phrase of your life?

## Positive Affirmation

*I am free.*

# Demeter

*Goddess of Grain and Harvest*

Archetype: Mother, Nurturer

*The hunger for love is much more difficult to remove than the hunger for bread.*
*– **Mother Teresa**[17]*

# WHO IS DEMETER?

As the goddess of grain and harvest, Demeter provides humanity with the ability to cultivate crops and she is responsible for the fruitfulness of nature. As Joseph Campbell said *"The Earth brings forth life, and the Earth nourishes life, and so is analogous to the powers of the woman"*[18]. In my interpretation of Demeter, she also symbolizes women who hold wells of nurturing love for others. Instinctively they express their love by offering physical or emotional nourishment, companionship and thoughtful care. Demeter is warm, compassionate and tends to give selflessly. All the good deeds in the world come from love, and love is the most prevailing force that exists. Therefore, by default, she is a powerful goddess.

Since I became a mother, I have a very different perspective when I read the news or watch a movie. If it is a tragic story, I often think there is nothing I wouldn't do to save my child. The urge to provide and to care for her is almost overwhelming. I never had that feeling before, as Demeter is not my natural archetype. She became increasingly active in me after my daughter was born. However, the transition began even in the early days of my pregnancy. I was more aware about the state of our natural environment, social-economic development and became more eager to make the world a better place.

The archetype of Demeter has in fact directly influenced me to write this book. In my early years, Athena was the most dominant archetype in me, then when I became fully immersed in the work of coaching individuals and later in purpose-driven businesses, the influence of Aphrodite grew increasingly strong in me. But when I became pregnant, I felt incredibly conscious of the mystical and miraculous power of being a woman. There was an inner calling to empower other women to actualize their potential, to support them to pursue their dreams. I know deep in my psyche that is an external projection and expansion of the same feeling that I have for my daughter, the willingness to do anything to help her to be the best she can be. That inner calling became the voice of this book, encouraging other women to discover their own mystical feminine power, and to emerge as powerful goddesses.

Therefore, the archetype of Demeter is more than a mother or a nurturer, it is part of her character, but there is something far greater than that. Demeter symbolizes the depth of the love we hold for one another, the capacity to care and inspire each other to be great, to be beautiful and to be powerful women.

## Archetype of a Mother and Nurturer

Apart from this deeper meaning of the Demeter archetype, we can identify other characteristics of this archetype. All mothers have some attributes of Demeter, but there are also women with or without children who tend to have more interest in entertaining at dinner parties, baking for charity events, or making homemade jam or bread. They are the natural providers, listeners and caretakers. You may have a friend you can count on to make you chicken soup when you are not well, or volunteer to help you whenever you are in need. Some Demeter women are very keen to tend an organic garden to grow earthy produce, and they will often share their harvest with friends and family. Demeter may not be an active archetype in you, but having a Demeter in your life is truly a blessing.

I met Rosemary at a social gathering at a friend's home many years ago. She arrived late because she was unwell, yet she brought with her big pots

of home cooked food, and dessert. We didn't get to talk much during the gathering, but when we were all leaving, I saw Rosemary helping another woman to load her bags into the car. Not only was Rosemary struggling with all her own big pots and boxes, she was also wearing some impossibly high heels. It was amusing to watch on one hand because I thought she would drop everything at any moment, but on the other hand, I made a note to myself that this woman is amazingly kind and generous in all regards. I didn't just stand there and watch, I did go help and that was the beginning of a long and wonderful friendship. The more I got to know Rosemary, the more I learned that Demeter is not limited to cooking big meals or looking after you when you are sick. She is someone who will be there to support and help you when she thinks she can be useful, with or without you knowing about it. She doesn't ask for quid pro quo or acknowledgement. She doesn't say *"what am I going to get out of this?"*. That is just not Demeter's line of thinking, she genuinely cares about the people she supports, regardless of whether she will receive anything in return.

Motherhood is a big one for Demeter. A young woman with a strong Demeter archetype may feel a strong urge to become a mother despite the circumstances being challenging. Equally, a woman who does not have any interest in raising a child may suddenly be drawn to starting a family when she enters a different stage in life when the influence of Demeter kicks in.

The energy that drives women to become mothers is very strong and it operates through a woman's psyche. When the Demeter archetype is fully activated, the chances are she will naturally fall pregnant, or she will be determined to do so. Often a Demeter woman wants to be married or at least in a committed and stable relationship in order to have a father for her children. Demeter wants the best for her children and therefore if she is mature and responsible, she will exercise control over her desire to become a mother. She will wait until the circumstances are suitable to raising a child, for instance when she is healthy, living conditions are stable and she has adequate energy to care for the baby.

We can all access the good mother within us, to take care of ourselves and do what is the best for us. Demeter can discern what is an act of self-love and what isn't. She can say yes to things when she wants them and, perhaps more importantly, she is able to say no to certain situations that is not good for her. However, this requires a Demeter who is highly conscious of her circumstances and her own wellbeing. Sometimes we find her more capable of being a good mother to others than to herself due to her altruistic character.

## Professional caretaker

The Demeter archetype is one that governs caretaking in general, so a Demeter woman might be drawn into a caretaker career. This is not limited to nurses or carers, it is any profession that supports wellbeing. Therefore, you may find a Demeter as a nutritionist, physiotherapist, teacher, author in health & wellbeing subjects, baker, chef, or an entrepreneur in health or baby products. The list is endless.

Demeter focuses on giving and service. She is, after all, the Great Mother. If that sense of giving and providing are driving everything you do, but you are a mortal woman with limited amounts of energy and resources, you can be susceptible to exhaustion. You may experience burnout and feel empty as you may neglect your own replenishment while you are too busy caring for others. The experience of burnout often happens to women whose major archetype is Demeter. It can happen quite easily when a Demeter woman has a demanding job and several children or family members to look after as well. As you can imagine, a Demeter tends to put everyone's well being before her own.

# Myths of Demeter

To fully understand the depth of Demeter, we must learn about her myths. She is the mother of Persephone (Maiden Goddess and Queen of the Underworld), the goddess of the next chapter. The story of "The Kidnapping of Persephone," is probably the most well-known myth about the bond between mother and daughter. The primary character in the myth is however, Demeter. In the story, Persephone was gathering narcissus flowers in the meadow. As a young and innocent maiden, the daughter of Demeter and Zeus, she lived a life of privilege. All that was on her mind was the beauty of the flowers and warmth of the sun and, accompanied by other nymphs and maiden goddesses, she noticed a particularly beautiful flower across the field. So she went over to pick it. Just as she reached down to pick this beautiful flower, the Earth opened up in front of her. Out of this deep, dark vent in the earth, the King of the Underworld, Hades, suddenly emerged on a chariot. He had come from the underworld specifically to take Persephone and he grabbed her in an instant and immediately went back underground. The Earth's surface closed up as if nothing has happened. The sun still shone and Persephone's company didn't notice a thing.

Underneath the Earth, it was a completely different story. Persephone screamed in terror as she had no idea what had just happened. She had been kidnapped by someone she didn't know and taken to a place where she had never been. It all happened in an instant. One moment Persephone had not a care in the world, and the next moment she found herself abducted into the Underworld.

Demeter on the other hand was carrying on with her day. Suddenly a sense that something had gone wrong came to her. This was perhaps due to that most powerful bond between two people, the psychic connection between a mother and her child.

Demeter sensed something was wrong with Persephone and so she went to the field where her daughter was supposed to be. She looked all over the field, but found no sign of Persephone. For the nine days and nine nights that followed, Demeter searched the world, but she couldn't find Persephone anywhere. She didn't sleep. She wouldn't eat or bathe. She was agitated, and worried sick for her daughter. She plunged into a deep depression. When that happened, the sky started to snow, the temperature dropped to freezing cold. The nine days felt like years on earth. Nothing could grow, there was no sign of life but only sorrow. All the harvest was gone and people starved.

Finally, the goddess of intuition, Hecate, came to help. She was known as the goddess of crossroads, as she could see three ways at once, and she offered her wisdom. Her three-way-perspective allowed her to see the past, present and future. She recalled that while in her cave, she heard Persephone scream, though she didn't see what happened. Hecate suggested going to Apollo, god of the Sun, who watched from above the Earth, as he might have seen what happened.

Hecate went with Demeter to Apollo, and sure enough, the god did see everything that had happened. He told them straightforwardly that Persephone had been abducted by Hades into the Underworld to be his bride. In fact, Apollo thought Hades was not bad for a son-in-law, after all, he was the King of the Underworld. On hearing this, Demeter became angry. Up to that point, Demeter had been depressed. Apollo saw Demeter's reaction, and so he added that Hades had asked for and received Zeus' permission for the wedding. He thought this information would settle the matter. But on the contrary, it only made Demeter more angry that without any discussion with Demeter or Persephone, Zeus had decided to let Hades take Persephone as his bride. At that point, Demeter was furious. The mother-daughter bond was clearly different from the father-daughter relationship in the Olympians' world.

Demeter was a powerful goddess in her own right, she was responsible for the fruitfulness of the harvest on Earth. She was once part of the Great Goddess that preceded the patriarchal gods, and for a long time, she was equated with the maternal aspect of the sacred feminine. She did not believe that Zeus' opinion took precedence, and did not accept his authority to give Persephone to Hades.

As Demeter grew more depressed and angry, her pain was reflected in the conditions on Earth. Unbearable weather and famine threatened the entire planet. Zeus realised that if all humans died, there would be no one to worship him. This motivated him to resolve the matter quickly. Zeus sent Hermes, the messenger god, to the Underworld and ordered Hades to return Persephone. Zeus promised Demeter that Persephone would be brought back very soon and this immediately eased her pain. The ice on earth started to melt and crops started to grow back.

Hermes went to fetch Persephone, however Persephone had no idea how long she would be kept in the Underworld. She was depressed and changed overnight from an innocent maiden to a mature woman goddess. This resonates with many women's experience of their very first emotional event, the sense that they don't know if they will ever feel the way they used to feel. When the darkness descends, there is no certainty about when or how the feeling will lift, or if the light will ever reappear. And that is how Persephone felt. She thought she would never see her mother, or the sun or the flowers again. She felt that she might never be in the Upperworld again and would be lost forever in the Underworld. This was an extremely challenging situation for a young innocent girl. Just when she was about to lose all hope, Hermes arrived with his chariot to fetch her.

Hermes explained all that happened in the Upperworld and that he was going to bring Persephone back to Demeter. Persephone was relieved, but before she left the Underworld, she had a moment with Hades. He offered her some pomegranate seeds to eat before the journey and she willingly ate them. Hermes then escorted the young goddess back to the light.

Demeter, who wasn't sure if she would ever see Persephone again, now rushed out of her temple, and Persephone, who never thought she would see her mother again, stepped off the chariot and ran to her mother. In one contemporary version of this myth, when the mother and daughter embraced, Earth came alive, and green grass and beautiful flowers started to blossom.

After their reunion, Demeter asked Persephone if she had eaten anything in the Underworld. Now, every properly raised young goddess, which Persephone certainly was, knew that if you ate anything in the Underworld, the Underworld would have a hold on you. Children learned never to eat anything from the Underworld. Reluctantly, Persephone told Demeter she did eat, but said Hades compelled her to do it. We all know that it wasn't true, but as far as the myth goes, young Persephone was not comfortable admitting her own action or owning it. The kidnapping had just sparked her transformation, she was still in the early stage of becoming what she would later be known as – the goddess of the Underworld.

Since Persephone had eaten six pomegranate seeds, she was forced to return to the Underworld periodically. She returned in the autumn after the crops had been harvested and stayed in the Underworld until spring when she was permitted to return to Upperworld, and her mother Demeter. In the myth, that is why the first signs of spring come with the greenness and flowers that appear on Earth each year when Persephone returns.

In this story, Demeter suffered as human beings suffer, and she is the only major divinity on Olympus that ever goes through this kind of emotional pain. This is one of the reasons she can relate to human suffering and why she cares so much for humanity.

## The myth of Demeter and Persephone

This myth about the abduction of Persephone has several levels of meaning. First of all, it demonstrates the level of desperation and devastation a mother feels when she is separated from her child or unable to help her loved one. In the story, Demeter is beside herself, everything around her is affected by her state of mind. Perhaps in more ways than we know, we are dependent on the mother figure or nurturer in our lives because we rely on having someone who cares about us that much.

Demeter is a powerful goddess and should be respected. Zeus may have underestimated her influence when he was inconsiderate of her feelings. That was clearly a mistake. This story reminds us not to take a Demeter for granted, no matter whether you are the Persephone or Zeus in the family. Sometimes we only know how much the Demeter in our lives means to us when she is sick or worse, gone.

Another insight offered by the story is the moment when Demeter accepts help from Hecate, the goddess of intuition, who is able to see through dimensions of time. Not only is it crucial for Demeter to ask for help, it also indicates the importance of being able to see different perspectives in this challenging situation, when Demeter is in disarray emotionally. In the next chapter, the deeper meaning of this myth for the archetype of Persephone is explored.

## Demeter daughter and mother

It may be rare, but it is possible to have a Demeter daughter and a Persephone mother. Although the attributes of a mother tend to develop more strongly when a woman has a child, it is also possible to be in a reverse situation when the mother in a family is not particularly nurturing or even quite absent due to health, work commitments or custody arrangement in a divorce. Sometimes the archetype of Demeter will emerge in a daughter if she needs to step up and look after her siblings even if the archetype is not naturally active in her. It may also apply to big families that have many children and the parents are both working full time. The older children often need to look after the younger ones in this scenario. The archetype in us can be a natural imprint but it can also be developed or activated due to circumstances.

## Relationships with Demeter

As Demeter is such a giver, it is easy to warm up a relationship with her in a family or as friends. In terms of romantic relationships, Demeter tends to be with someone who loves being cared for, or someone who admires her kindness and fully supports her endeavours. Often it is clear that a Demeter would like to have children, even if it will be years later. The need to provide and nurture is very strong in a Demeter, if she is unable to conceive naturally she is willing to go the extra mile to do so, or she may decide to adopt. If a Demeter has a miscarriage or abortion, the pain will be very deep and it may take quite some time for healing to take place. It is important to give her time and support as this is very hard for a Demeter to process.

If a Demeter does not end up having children, she may work with children or in other helping professions. The experience of nurturing and loving is not limited to having her own children. A Demeter may dream of creating a non-profit for single mothers who are struggling, or a clinic for children who have health problems. She will blossom when the business or project is able to help people, but she will be devastated if it doesn't work out. One way or the other, we find Demeter is often surrounded by people and she forms authentic heartfelt relationships with them.

## What can we learn from Demeter

Demeter is like the sun, she radiates and warms our hearts. She cares deeply and takes things personally for that very reason. There is nothing wrong with being personal, in fact modern business culture can be too transactional and often modern relationships are overly digital. Demeter reminds us about the virtue of selfless service, the importance of using our talents or gifts to contribute to the greater good. If we work with a Demeter in business, we know she will take good care of people, because she knows the treatment people receive matters a lot. In social setting, Demeter will be the one who is most helpful, the one who listens and fully engages in conversations.

Lately I have noticed a new phenomenon emerging, more and more women are speaking up and showing up to make a collective effort towards social justice, moral standards and environmental protection. I believe many of us feel a fierce protective instinct towards our own children and our home, and it extends to the children of the world and our own Planet Earth. Women who may have another archetype, such as Artemis, naturally active in them may adopt a more Demeter sensitivity given the current increasingly divisive social and political climate. As I mentioned before, I didn't think I had much Demeter in me naturally, but since becoming a mother, I have gained a sense of empathy towards other children and people in need that I have never felt before. It is as if my biochemistry has changed and I am more reactive and responsive towards issues that concern people in war zones and our future generations. There are trajectories for our collective future, one is towards decline if we allow more wars, poverty, hatred and environmental degradation to happen. The other trajectory points to more awakening, activism and positive changes that are triggered by the collective realization of our current state of world affairs. Demeter women will answer the call and rise up to be the mothers of the world.

## Ways to grow beyond

With her generous nature, Demeter is more susceptible to burnout than other archetypes, as she tends to take responsibilities for too many things and probably for far too many people. This is probably not a surprise given her attributes. It is different from being a so-called 'People Pleaser' because she is not motivated by people's opinion about her, it is her innate nature that drives her to provide or to help. When a Demeter is exhausted and empty, it may be hard for her to continue to do what she wants to do and she will find herself feeling frustrated or depressed. Over time, if she does not properly communicate her feelings, she may even develop a sense of resentment, feeling that no one acknowledges her sacrifices or fully understands her needs.

A Demeter needs regular "recharging" physically and emotionally. It is important for her to know what nurtures her and what her heart truly desires. Sometimes a Demeter gets too busy focusing on others and forgets her own needs until something stops her in her tracks, like falling ill, which is not uncommon for an overworked Demeter. Having a healthy sense of self-care is vital for the wellbeing of a Demeter.

If a Demeter find herself unable to say no to the needs of other people, she needs to learn the difference between providing for genuine needs and keeping somebody dependent because of her own need to be a provider. The danger here is that she will develop codependent relationships with people.

A Demeter should also be mindful of how she responds to unreasonable requests. If someone succeeds in making a Demeter feel guilty because she doesn't want to help she is giving herself away too easily. She needs to become aware of that tendency. As mentioned earlier, love often leads us to say 'yes', but sometimes it is actually a more loving response to be able to say 'no'.

Another challenge for a Demeter is learning to let go. If someone or something disappoints Demeter and she becomes bitter and feeling victimized, she will need to develop the willingness to see the situation differently and be able to rise above the situation. Otherwise she may stay resentful emotionally and find it hard to move on.

# Self-care for Demeter

## Aromatherapy

Demeter loves to provide, care and give to others. This means that Demeter's blend should include lavender and geranium oil. You could also add any of the other herbaceous florals to her blend. Everlasting oil would also be a perfect addition. We should also add a little seed oil – preferably something sweeter such as coriander seed and a dash of sweet orange to balance it out.

*For more information on Aromatherapy and the Goddesses, please refer to Appendix 1.

## Wellbeing practices

The top priority of self-care for a Demeter is to become a good mother to herself.

She must do what nurtures her body and soul: A hearty, healthy meal? A massage? A quiet weekend? A walk on the beach? A Demeter should make a date with herself for some 'me time'.

- Meditation – to practice stillness and develop a sense of inner peace.
- Yoga – a great way to connect body and mind, and an opportunity to become more body aware and to develop the ability to listen to the body's need.
- Journaling – helpful for people who habitually bottle up feelings.
- Time off – at the next friends-get-together, try a restaurant or cafe and skip all the cooking and preparation!

## ❝Note-to-self:

> *"Being extremely honest with oneself is a good exercise"*
> – Sigmund Freud

> *"When the well is dry, we know the worth of water."*
> – Benjamin Franklin

## Self-reflective questions

Whether you are a Demeter or not, these self-care questions can help you become more aware of the things that will bring you clarity and comfort. They can also help you find answers that will replenish and nurture your soul.

- What does your body need to feel nurtured, strong and healthy?
- What kind of food do you need?
- Are you taking supplements or herbs?
- Are you getting adequate sleep?
- What kind of exercise is your body yearning for?
- Who can give you support when you are afraid or need help?

- Who comforts you, makes you feel safe and allows you to have your feelings?
- Who do you need to avoid? Who adds to your anxiety level or overwhelms you?
- Is there a support group (friends, meditation circle, coaching group, etc.) that you can turn to?
- What's your best healthy distraction to take a break from emotional stress?
- What unhelpful coping strategies or activities do you need to avoid?
- What responsibilities or commitments do you need to release to clear some space?
- How can you best express your emotions?
- What will help you be more present and at peace?
- What do you need to do in order to get quiet time just for yourself?
- What kind of spiritual practice helps you to connect with God and your soul?
- What can you do to bring more comfort into your life at this time?

## Positive Affirmation

*I am open to give and to receive love.*

# PERSEPHONE

## *Maiden & Goddess of Underworld*

Archetype: The Mystic

*The Princess does become a queen if she stays the road.*
*– A Woman's Worth,* **Marianne Williamson**

# Who is Persephone?

A young Persephone is innocent, carefree and sensitive in nature. She tends to be quiet as she observes what is happening around her and forms her opinion which she may not necessarily share with the outer world. She may come across as introverted and quiet, especially when she is young. There is something eternally youthful in a Persephone, no matter her age, you can see it in her eyes or smile. As we have become acquainted with Persephone in the last chapter, we know the kidnapping story in her myth. In real life, I find most Persephone women experience a significant event when they are young, which often triggers a rapid transition into becoming a mature woman. Sometimes the cause is due to the break up of a relationship, relocation, parents' divorce, abuse, illness or financial crisis in the family, or if they witness or personally suffer from a tragic or traumatic event. No matter the cause, it greatly affects a Persephone mentally and emotionally. Everyone has their own coping mechanisms and the period of transition and emotional healing varies from person to person. However, when a Persephone emerges from a challenging time, she will not be the innocent and carefree maiden goddess any longer.

I met Ruby at one of my goddess workshops a few years back. Although she was in her mid-fifties, Ruby had sparkling blues eyes, rosy cheeks and an almost childlike smile. She wore a silk top that resembled a Kandinsky painting that day. She made such a strong impression on me that I can still remember her appearance vividly. At the end of my workshop, she came to tell me that her life story exactly followed my description of the Persephone myth. After a series of traumatic events and abuse in her teenage years, she was lost, ill and depressed for a long time. Eventually she embarked on her healing journey and came to discover a deeper sense of meaning and purpose in life. Since then she has been teaching art therapy as a way to help others to heal.

Ruby is a beautiful embodiment of the Persephone archetype who eventually actualized her feminine power despite the adversity in her early years. I was really touched by her journey and the eternal youthfulness in her smile. My impression of her has since been superimposed onto my vision of Persephone. In fact, I have met many more Persephone women since Ruby and many of them have been older women. They all share similar characteristics and personal history, but most importantly of all, they all have triumphed over their tears.

As Marianne Williamson said it in her book, *A Woman's Worth*, "*there are millions of girls who are depressed to a degree beyond what their families and friends find normal, but who are actually undergoing the feminine journey into full and actualized consciousness. One day they will be queens, and the transition wouldn't have happened had they not cracked up when they did*". There are many young Persephones among us and around us, sometimes we don't even know they are undergoing such transformation.

As the media idealizes certain images of women, there is an increasing pressure for women to to look and behave in a certain way to fit into narrow roles. Social media may help to connect people through cyberspace, but at the same time the endless amount of information and opinion can amount to an overwhelming pressure, specially for young women. The digital age can be a very confusing time for a young Persephone as the question of who she is tends to get lost in the idea of who she should be.

The transition from a young girl to a grown woman is a process of self-discovery, and it is in constant interaction with the world. This process takes Persephone into uncharted territory, and it is both exciting and frightening at times. Without a strong support network like family or friends, it can be a very difficult time. This is a transformation that involves both body and mind, and it cannot be forced but must be respected. When the Persephone archetype faces a dramatic event in her adolescence, it catalyzes this transformation, and so it is often intense. If a Persephone makes the choice to get through the experience instead of suppressing it, she will emerge as the goddess she was always meant to be: powerful, intuitive and with an incredible ability to guide others.

# Myths of Persephone

Before we dive deeper into this archetype, it is worthwhile revisiting the underlying meaning of the "The Kidnapping of Persephone" myth.

In the myth the King of Underworld, Hades, abducts Persephone, but this is a marriage arranged with Zeus' permission. So in the patriarchal rules of Olympia, since Zeus agrees to the marriage, everybody else is supposed to adjust to the arrangement, including Demeter and Persephone. But Demeter is furious with Zeus' secret decision and the innocent Persephone is simply shocked about her change of fate.

The maiden phase is a part of a girl's life identified by many cultures. In this myth, Persephone is her mother's daughter, and they share a close bond. Her archetypal tendencies are to be fairly indefinite; that is, there is a pleasant quality about her, she is easygoing and hardly causes any trouble. She is often seen as a beautiful woman, with a gentle and receptive feminine energy about her. Maybe this is why Zeus thought she would have no problem accepting the arranged marriage.

However the most significant aspect of Persephone's myth is her transformation, changing from an innocent maiden goddess, living a carefree day in the Upper world admiring a narcissus, to suddenly being abducted to the Underworld, while the rest of the world continues as if nothing has happened.

There are many examples in life of times when the rug is suddenly pulled from under you and you find yourself in a descent of the psyche. A health issue, an unanticipated financial crisis, the sudden end of a relationship, are among many things can unexpectedly go wrong for people. Out of the blue, your world is dimmed by fear. Everything may look fine on the surface but it's not, especially not within you.

The classic story of Persephone is that the flower that she reached for was either a poppy or a narcissus. As the key ingredient of opium, poppy is an image of substance abuse and the draw of the underworld. Narcissus is about self-esteem and the experiences in life that cultivate a healthy sense of self. Both flowers hold strong symbolic meaning in Persephone's myth.

The Underworld symbolizes the unconscious part of our psyche, and it contains our intuition, our inner knowing within ourselves. After her reunion with Demeter in the Upper world and the realization that she will need to return to the Underworld for half of the year, Persephone eventually accepts the consequence of her actions. Had she not eaten the pomegranate seeds, the Underworld wouldn't have a hold on her and she wouldn't need to return. This incident symbolizes the development of one's own sexuality. At first sexuality hasn't been very alive in her, as she was young and innocent. But as she matures, she eventually becomes the queen who rules by Hades' side. Over time, she becomes the guide of the newly dead souls in the Underworld, and she helps them to find their way in the afterlife. She has grown and earned her power. Persephone has truly transformed.

Persephone is often depicted with a pomegranate in paintings because of the myth, and this fruit also symbolizes fertility as it has many seeds. Interestingly, Aphrodite also shares the pomegranate symbol, and in fact, this goddess of beauty who is known for her passionate liaisons is tangled in a myth with Persephone over a mortal lover, Adonis.

Adonis was a remarkable, handsome young man who was adored by Aphrodite. In order to keep him away from her husband Hephaestus, the god of metalsmiths and stonemasonry, Aphrodite hid her lover in a box and asked Persephone to look after him in the Underworld. This plan didn't work out so well when Persephone fell in love with Adonis herself and refused to return him to Aphrodite. Both goddesses wanted to continue their affairs with Adonis and eventually they asked Zeus to decide who should have Adonis. Since both were fighting to win Adonis, Zeus decided that Adonis would spend a third of the year with Persephone, a third with Aphrodite and keep a third to his own disposal. Moral issues aside, as both goddesses were married and Adonis being a mortal, didn't seem to have any say in this matter. The myth shows that Persephone is not an innocent and carefree daughter any more. She has become a goddess who knows what she wants and is not afraid to ask or even fight for it. This myth demonstrates the change in Persephone from her earlier myth, she is no longer helpless and fearful, she is in charge of her own passion and asserts her own power.

# Archetype of a mystic

The Persephone archetype tends to be introverted and intuitive. A young Persephone can sense what others are thinking or feeling. She tends to go along with what's expected of her. Even though she has a mind of her own, she may not necessarily express her inner thoughts or wishes. She enjoys being in the company of extroverted people and she is often attracted to confident and mature men.

A young Persephone often has difficulties with boundaries, perhaps because she may have a mother who likes to take care of everything for her, which prevents a certain level of autonomy and individuality in the daughter. As a young girl enters adolescence, there's something about becoming who you are that includes keeping secrets. It means having an inner life, and if you are a Persephone, the tendency to start to differentiate yourself from your parents' image of you can become quite apparent.

As a non-dominating maiden goddess, Persephone can incorporate all the other goddess archetypes and so she may become a much more complex personality as she matures. Persephone's ultimate identity depends upon her individual story and the decisions she makes.

## CAREER FOR PERSEPHONE

Not every woman with a Persephone archetype has to be abducted into the Underworld, or endure a traumatic event in her early life. But she does tend to have a knowledge of the Underworld, the unconscious mind, and she is often highly intuitive and may even have psychic abilities. A Persephone has the sense of being able to know something about the in-between worlds and the darker sides of things as well. She enjoys working with her intuition in whatever field she chooses. She may also work as a psychic or a healer if she decides to develop this ability professionally.

A Persephone may become a musician, artist, poet or writer in any form, as creative work gives her an avenue to express her inner world and she has a natural ability to go very deep within herself.

If she is a therapist, she is particularly adept at working with people experiencing mental and emotional challenges. She understands them and relates to them. She knows how to tap into the unconscious mind and she can help people to navigate their journeys and begin their healing. This ability can make her a very gifted therapist or healer who can draw from the deeper levels in the personal and collective unconscious.

## PERSEPHONE DAUGHTER AND MOTHER

If a Persephone has a Demeter mother, her mother takes great care of her and may even makes decisions for her. If she has an Artemis mother, she may disappoint her mother because she may not be as passionate or persistent in her pursuits. If she has an Athena mother, her mother may wish her to be more assertive or decisive. She may not be indecisive, but may be uncertain or unconfident about her own opinions. The Persephone archetype does not naturally have a big personality and often archetypes like Athena or Artemis may cast a shadow on her in the family.

If Persephone is the mother and her daughter has a strong archetype such as Athena or Artemis, the daughter will become very independent young in life and want to have a say in everything. In fact, the daughter may even get frustrated with her mild-mannered mother and try to make decisions for her mother. A Persephone mother won't challenge her daughter because Persephone tends to avoid confrontations and promotes harmony. A Persephone can understand other people's perspectives and how to resolve situations with fluidity, flexibility and creativity. She doesn't move forward with brute force of will or effort, but flows with feminine receptivity, sensitivity and sensibility in any challenging situation. She may take some time to achieve her goals, but she prefers this to direct conflict.

## Relationships with Persephone

Since a Persephone tends to be attractive, agreeable and pleasant, she often fits the image of the princess, or the ideal of a young woman. Naturally, not only will maternal figures want to mother a Persephone, but many different men are likely to be attracted to her as their idealized feminine partner as well.

If a Persephone is attracted to a man and he projects his ideal image onto her, and if she acts in accordance with this, people may see her through that projection. In other words, she may take on a chameleon-like quality. She unconsciously shifts and becomes the woman that this particular man expects her to be. She becomes interested in his interests. She dresses the way he likes to see her. She behaves as he wants her to behave, often based on his assumptions of who she is. A young Persephone may have an unconscious tendency to please other people and to conform to their expectations or their projections. This may be one way to avoid tension but it also delays revealing her true identity.

Persephone's problem, before she finds the strength and confidence to project her true identity, is that she is drawn to people who are attracted to her without examining whether she is attracted to them. In this scenario, she may even marry someone simply because everyone else wants her to, without knowing if she really wants to commit to her husband. This kind of marriage may also be very difficult for the husband because she isn't fully committed mentally or emotionally. He may feel a sense of her absence while she may feel she is a captive in his world. This scenario is more likely to occur if a Persephone marries young.

This kind of situation can have profound effects, especially as a woman engages with her sexuality. When a woman who has not felt sexual even though she has been seen as a desirable object by men, comes into her sexuality later in life, things can change with her partner.

They can go one of two ways. In some marriages, something shifts in the woman and in the man over time. What started out as a one-sided marriage, where he chose her and she went along with it, can grow closer physically and emotionally as the couple goes through life experiences together. In other marriages, when a Persephone matures and finds her own voice, her husband may not necessarily be compatible with the woman she has become. In these cases, the couple will find their marriage becomes challenging.

However, in a different scenario, if a man proposes marriage to a young Persephone, she may decide to break off the relationship. She may be unable to commit because she feels the need to discover her strength and purpose instead of just responding to everyone else's expectations of her. People may be surprised, but when she makes it through, she will be stronger and will be a great example of personal transformation.

## What can we learn from Persephone

Persephone is someone who can survive a deep descent. When she makes it through that tunnel, she is stronger and more motivated through finding a deeper meaning in her life. The Persephone archetype represents a woman who has within herself the receptivity of someone who will no longer be victimized, it is like the new spring after the winter, there is a feeling of new beginnings and possibilities.

Persephone is an archetype that resembles the eternal maiden, and she represents the first part of a woman's adulthood, when she may hesitate to make commitments or big decisions in her relationships or career. She may feel that although she loves a person or a job, she fears if she makes a commitment she may miss other opportunities. She's often a talented person who does well at a number of things, but there's always a sense of fear of missing out. Often there have been some difficult experiences in a Persephone's past that she has covered over which can influence her fear of commitment.

Also a Persephone woman avoids anger. She does not want people to get angry with her. She may suppress her true desire. She may experience emotional challenges as a turning point in her life, which may have positive or negative consequences. These may mark the beginning of recurring issues, or she may overcome the challenges and they may mark the beginning of maturity. These moments come when there is no choice but to take full responsibility for one's life. It starts a process of maturing that may not have happened before. A classic example of this dynamic is the relationship between a stage-manager mother and an actress daughter. When the daughter is ready to become a mature goddess, she overthrows her mother's desires and claims what she wants. This aspect of the Persephone archetype develops, as in the myth, as a result of difficult experiences and growth.

Symbolically, the Underworld can represent deeper layers of the psyche, a place where memories and feelings have been "buried" (the personal unconscious) and where images, patterns, instincts, and feelings that are archetypal and shared by humanity are found. Persephone, as the Queen of the Underworld, represents the ability to move back and forth between the ego-based reality and the more conscious, spiritually grounded understanding of the world around us.

Growing up, Persephone tends to be vulnerable to addiction as she may want to withdraw from the world. But when you see Persephone acting as a guide for others, it indicates that she has found her way around the inner world, and she has gained wisdom through the lessons learned from the outer world. During this process, it may have appeared that she wasn't actively doing anything in her life, but Persephone is the observer, taking it all in, until the point, when she steps up with her knowledge, and comes into her own as Queen of the Underworld.

Persephone doesn't have a particularly negative shadow like some of the stronger archetypes which cause other people problems, therefore she needs to look harder at the impact of her shadow on herself. Persephone in therapy can be difficult on the therapist because of a lack of definition in her character.

If you had a Persephone mother as a child, or at the beginning your life was hard, and you had to take care of yourself, you may have had to suppress the archetype of Persephone. Sometimes women say it's never too late to have a happy childhood. As an adult woman, even at a grandmother stage of life, you may finally be able to spend quality time with your soul friends, your sisterhood or even your boyfriends. You may go out and play, the equivalent of looking at the pretty flowers in the myth. You may travel, go to the theatre, try new things like social dancing. The Persephone archetype can develop in your later years, like your 50s, 60s, 70s and so on, if you never had a chance to do develop it when you were younger.

## Ways to grow beyond

Persephone can be one of the more difficult of the archetypes because of her indefiniteness. She can show up more clearly somewhere around the ages of 35 to 45 when there is dissatisfaction, a sense of missing out on life. When eternally youthful Persephone reaches that age, she gets to a point where reluctance to settle down doesn't work anymore. There is the realization that it is time for commitment. She actually may know what attracts her, but may be afraid to follow it. Perhaps it is the desire to develop psychic abilities or become a healer or do something more creative. She may feel a desire to find her purpose in work or causes, or her yearning for commitment can be about relationships or starting a family. Her soul calls for greater acknowledgement, and the calling in her heart can become stronger and harder to ignore when a Persephone grows more mature through life experience.

A crucial point in Persephone's myth is the moment when she tells her mother that she ate the pomegranate seeds because Hades compelled her. A mature Persphone will now own her decisions, if she wants to change her circumstances. It takes personal courage to make a step in the direction of one's own individuality, and not everyone is willing to answer that call.

When Persephone enters a different stage in life, it can be through marriage or perhaps motherhood, the transition will inevitably lead to some form of self-reflection. If a Persephone is not happy or fulfilled, she will question what truly matters in her heart and who she actually wants to become. Sometimes all we need to do is to sit with these questions, connect and centre, and listen to to what our inner goddesses have to say.

If other archetypes get activated at this time, for example, if she becomes pregnant, Demeter may take a stronger hold on her and she will find meaning and purpose in being a mother. If she finds herself deepening into the role of a wife and experiences satisfaction in that, the Hera archetype will be gaining influence on her. These influences from other archetypes may be temporary or more permanent but, regardless, it is about finding deeper meaning in life.

Persephone also needs to learn something about negotiating honestly between tensions. Knowing what she wants and, maybe with Athena's help and strategy, she can figure out a way to achieve it without going along with things she wouldn't have chosen herself.

If a Persephone doesn't learn something about growing up in life, she will become that woman in later years who still behaves with a certain coyness, like a girl who never became a woman. It's the Persephone who stayed stuck in the role of the eternal maiden. To grow, a Persephone woman must individuate, be assertive, consciously make commitments and live up to them. It may mean gaining the confidence and courage to trust that she is a powerful goddess.

# Self-care for Persephone

## Aromatherapy

Persephone has an eternal youthfulness. She is the queen of the underworld. She knows what she wants, is very intuitive and tends to be interested in spiritual matters. A rich earthy and woody blend would be perfect along with florals and resins. Persephone's blend should have patchouli, vetiver, frankincense, rose absolute with some fresh citrus oils to balance it.

*For more information on Aromatherapy and the Goddesses, please refer to Appendix 1.*

## Well-being practices

Persephone has a natural tendency to go deep within and so it is actually helpful to spend some time outdoors to connect with nature, get warm under the sun and to move physically.

- Physical exercises – any movement activity that you enjoy.
- Meditation – to quiet the mind and connect with inner wisdom.
- Gratitude journal – write down what you appreciate and are grateful for every day.

- ❧ Self-examination – recognize negative self-talk and be willing to change your perspective.
- ❧ Learning – read or listen to inspirational books/audios.
- ❧ Goals – set them and commit to achieving them, consider working with a coach.

## ❝ Note-to-self:

*"Our deepest fear is not that we are inadequate. Our deepest fear is that we are powerful beyond measure. It is our light, not our darkness, that most frightens us."*
– *A Return to Love*, Marianne Williamson

*"Litten girls with dreams become women with vision"*
– unknown

## Self-reflective questions

You may like to answer these self-reflective questions as you read through this book or schedule some quiet time in your week to focus on going within. It may be a nice way to prepare yourself by doing a 10 to 15-minute meditation before writing down your thoughts. There are no rules; whichever ways can help you to connect with your inner self will be beneficial to you.

- ❧ Recall yourself as a child and adolescent, were you a Persephone? What are some of the qualities or experiences that you have that match with Persephone? Or is someone you know a Persephone?

- What of your mother, was she a Persephone? If so, was there a role reversal, did you take care of her?
- Recall the times when you were a Persephone taken into the Underworld (it happens to everyone). Your life was going smoothly, and suddenly it changed; someone or something you counted on got torn away from you and you were in the Underworld. This comes with sudden news about loss, disillusion, betrayal, and events that destroy your assumptions about your good health, job, relationships, home or financial security. Perhaps you were in denial, and you couldn't sustain certain illusions any more. No matter how it happened, you found yourself in the Underworld.
- What was your experience?
- How did you get through this phase and back into the Upper world?
- How did it affect you? What are your lessons learned?
- Did your spirituality deepen or lessen? If so, in what way?

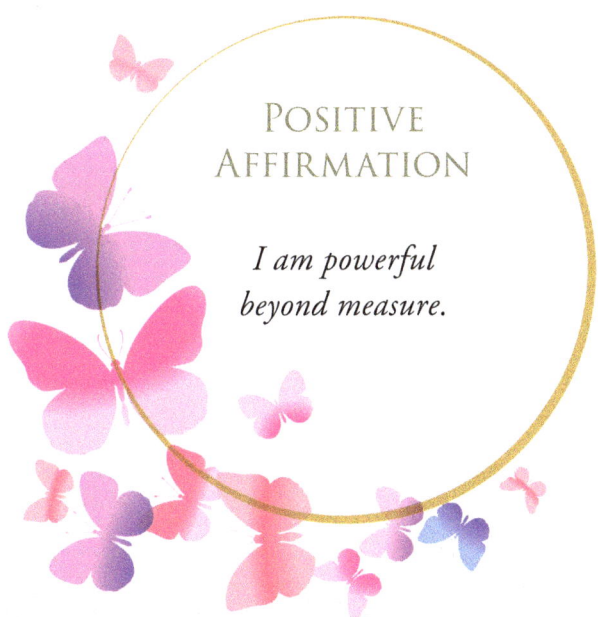

## Positive Affirmation

*I am powerful beyond measure.*

# HERA

*Goddess of Marriage and Queen of Olympia*

Archetype: The Queen

*The purpose of life as a woman is to ascend to the throne and rule with heart.*
*– A Woman's Worth,* **Marianne Williamson**

## Who is Hera?

Up until about 60 years ago, many girls and women aspired to the Hera archetype.

Think of the world of Jane Austen for example. In any kind of aristocracy, a woman needed a well-established husband if she wanted to live well or have an influential position in society. Women at that time had no right to vote or to own land under their own names. The importance of women marrying, and marrying well, was strongly built into the culture and collective psyche for a long time.

Even in highly industrialised countries, in the 1950s most women who managed to go to university considered marriage to be the next logical next step. Then came the '60s and '70s, and the idea of marriage as an institution changed dramatically. Today, women in most developed countries have options: to marry, stay single, or put the decision off for now. There is an assumption that we will prioritise our education, then work and career, though there will be relationships during these years. Many women now do not depend on a partner or a husband to support them. This is a big shift in modern culture and Hera, the archetype of marriage, is changing with the times as well.

Although I must point out sadly that there are still small parts of the world where a woman's worth remains strongly dependent on being married for social and economic status, for a place to live and for food, in most parts of the world, women now have means to be independent. But there are certainly some women who are hardwired with the Hera archetype in their psyche. They choose to marry young because they want to, not because they need to. Some may even dream about a lavish wedding when they are still teenagers. Some women however, desire marriage, but prefer to wait until they are more established in life, for example with more financial security. These women typically do not wish to live with a partner or have children until after marriage. The influence of Hera starts emerging when a woman becomes ready to settle down. She may also want to start a family and feels that getting married is a prerequisite.

I personally can relate to that sudden emergence of the Hera archetype. In my late teens early twenties I was dating an intelligent young man. My mother adored him and everyone thought he was the perfect guy. But I could not possibly imagine "settling down" so early in life, let alone getting married. Then I went through a period of dating many different types of men, followed by a period of no one at all. I have experienced long-distance relationships, as well as short-term, long-term, undefined and ambiguous and monumental ones. I have made mistakes and I have learned lessons. I had some good laughs and I have shed tears too. Still, I never contemplated the word marriage or a dream-like wedding. I just didn't think about this concept at all. I didn't like to be asked "Where is this relationship going?". I used to say, "It goes where it needs to go!". I disliked the "deadline" pressure and the confrontation. If something is serious, you know. If you don't know, it just means you don't want to know the truth.

Then, in 2012, I started to date my husband, and everything fell into place. It just felt right. Somewhere between the second and third year into our relationship, out of the blue I had this feeling: it is time. I liked the idea of getting married. Just like that. I wanted to honour the sacred commitment and the bond between the two of us.

Regardless of what triggers the Hera archetype to emerge or become active, she signifies someone who honours and acknowledges a sacred commitment. She is loyal and willing to be part of a lifelong partnership that can move through challenges and celebrations. She thrives in a committed relationship.

When a Hera walks in the door, she lights up the room. There is a queen-like quality and elegance to her. She is poised, gracious and attentive. Men find her attractive and appreciate her feminine appearance. She doesn't intimidate or dominate and it is very pleasant to have a conversation with her. She can hold her place among strong and powerful people, because above all, she is the Queen of Olympia.

## Myths of Hera

To fully understand the Hera archetype, first we need to know something about her myths. Hera, the Goddess of Marriage is also the result of a major cultural shift. Beginning around 4000 BC, the first influx of Indo-European tribes, warrior people with masculine war-orientated mythology, invaded the agricultural tribes of Mesopotamia and Southeast Asia. These invaded peoples were planters and herders with a primarily matriarchal culture. The warrior people came in waves, bringing their patriarchal society and patriarchal religions with them[19]. The planters had no chance against the warrior raiders and the whole culture changed with the matriarchy slowly fading.

What the warrior people didn't destroy, they stole. They settled among the agricultural goddess-worshipping people, marrying into their communities. In parallel with the human reality, the powerful male deities began to either overpower the local goddesses, or to marry them. The chief patron gods were thunder-hurlers, very much like the warrior peoples themselves, such as Zeus and Thor, among others. This is one reason why Zeus had so many affairs, he married a goddess in one valley, and when the tribe conquered the next valley, he married another goddess. Over time the culture began to unify all these areas and Zeus developed a long history of affairs[20].

As a result, other Earth and divine feminine power were diminished by the sky gods and warrior gods and often the goddesses became consorts of the gods. Hera, known as the Great Goddess, and sometimes the the Triple Goddess, was Maiden, Mother and Crone, all in one. She was the goddess who provided and nurtured during the time of the goddess culture. Later with the conquest of patriarchy she became known as the Queen of Olympia, ruling besides Zeus.

Hera shared a genealogy with the rest of the Olympians, she was the daughter of Gaia and Cronus, liberated when Zeus overthrew Cronus, who had done the same to his father, Uranus. So now we have the lineage of the patriarchy, where the head of power is often restless and fearful of his sons who may overthrow him. This is a very different collective psyche to one with an abundant mother as the head of the family or tribe, who gives birth to her divine children and nurtures them in life. As in the old saying that it takes a village to raise a child, there is a sense of cooperation, collaboration and connection in the matriarchal environment. The heart of the effort of the society is for the greater good, while in the patriarchy, power sits with the leaders or rulers of the time.

In the myth of Zeus and Hera, Zeus, being the chief of gods of Olympus, is attracted to Hera's beauty. He courts Hera without success for 300 years. He sets her as his greatest challenge, and uses his shape-shifting ability to seduce her. Zeus transforms himself into a bull, then into a shower of gold, and a number of others things. Eventually he shapeshifts into a bird shivering in cold in order to gain Hera's sympathy. Hera sees this chilled little bird and picks it up and puts it between her breasts to warm. Once the little bird, who is of course Zeus, gets this close to Hera, he transforms back into his real form and assumes that he can possess her sexually. But she as an Olympian, also has power. She says to him "Not until you marry me." So this is how Zeus gets Hera's hand in marriage.

Many women in history, and some still today, have followed Hera's example in putting off a man who wants premarital sex. Hera is clear and firm. She is an Olympian herself and she demands that her wishes are honoured and respected.

In one version of the myth, Hera and Zeus have a honeymoon that lasts 300 years, but when it is over, it is really over. Zeus is involved in numerous affairs and has many children with other goddesses. Hera, the bride and the wife who fulfils her meaning as an archetype in the first period of marriage later becomes the archetype of the vindictive woman. This is how we often find her in the mythology of storytellers like Homer. Hera has received a bad reputation that she may not necessary deserve.

First, as pointed out earlier, the Greek mythologies we are familiar with today have come from the patriarchal period when the gods dominated and asserted their power to diminish the divine feminine, the goddesses. So it's no surprise that many of the myths painted an angry and jealous image of Hera reacting to Zeus' numerous betrayals. Whether this implies that she should accept her husband's affairs, rather than getting angry, is hard to say. This may be compared to the Kidnapping of Persephone myth, in which none of the gods considered it inappropriate to abduct Persephone.

An archetype is like a mould, a pattern, that we can identify in our collective psyche. We know one when we see one. Archetypes are universal, so the image of Hera can be found in various cultures, geographies, races and times. She does not suffer in silence, but speaks up and asks to be respected.

In the modern world, as the idea of marriage and the balance of power between men and women changes, the archetype of Hera is also changing. She has evolved and grown to reflect our modern values.

As a goddess, Hera was ritually honoured by women. In a carryover of the pre-patriarchal rites, women maintained their allegiance to feminine divinities. In the spring, Hera was worshiped as the Maiden. In summer, Hera was the Perfected One. Then in the autumn, she was Hera the Widow, when Zeus began to pursue other goddesses. In winter, due to those terrible betrayals and her great grief, Hera was said to disappear into the woods. She went into the darkness where she wandered over the whole Earth in grief. Then when spring returned, Hera was worshipped with a spring ritual. A statue of her was immersed in a spring or pool of water, and she became Hera the virgin again. So in a sense, Hera goes through a whole cycle with the seasons, and the immersion into water allows her to emerge once again as the virgin. Metaphorically she goes on an emotional journey, experiencing pain and disappointment, grief and suffering, but eventually she is healed and renewed.

The tradition of getting married in June is a tradition that goes back to the times of Hera. To the Romans her name was Juno, and the month of June is named after her. Zeus, which means 'bringer to completion', and Hera entered their sacred marriage in a ritual that perfected or completed her.

Hera and Zeus had two sons. Hephaestus was the imperfect child with a clubfoot who became a skilled blacksmith and craftsman creating beautiful things, musical instruments and weapons for war. He was raised by nymphs of the sea who taught him how to make things with his hands and with his forge. Their other son was Ares, the god of war.

The characters of children can sometimes be considered an extension of their parents. Hera has two pretty colourless daughters who are not goddesses but minor divinities with a ferocity like a force of nature such as a cyclone. When Zeus seduces a mortal girl named Aegina, who gave her name to the Aegina Island, it's said that Hera, in her wrath, destroyed the entire population of the island with a cyclone. Whether this myth is again a way to depict Hera as an angry and temperamental wife, is subject to debate. What is certain is that Hera is a powerful deity who is should not be disrespected or ignored.

## Archetype of a Queen

Historically, there has been an assumption that marriage will bring fullness, completeness or perfection to women, especially in cultures where marriage meant having a role in society, being accepted, protected and taken care of. Little girls wanted to become a beautiful bride and wanted to become a valued wife. This assumption had more relevance and truth in the past. With changing of times, the archetype is being expressed in our psyche and behaviour in new ways.

What remains true is that the high point of Hera's story is the union of marriage, and it is also the high point of the archetype, the sense of being perfected by a union with the divine spouse in a sacred marriage.

In the Jungian world, the sacred marriage is often referred to as the inner marriage between the masculine and feminine that is inherently in all of us. As the Wooglers put it, *"The archetypal masculine mode of consciousness has more historically to be associated with linear thinking, intellect, reason, Logos; the archetypal feminine mode of consciousness with analogical thinking, intuition, feeling, Eros."*[21] We need both to be whole. A woman in most circumstances will predominantly possess the feminine mode of consciousness, especially in a relationship. But when a woman needs to use more thinking than feeling in certain situations, such as at the workplace, she can switch to use her masculine mode of consciousness too. To be whole, we need to be able to balance both energies and use both modes. The best way to sum it up is *"thoughts without content are empty; and intuitions without concepts blind."*[22]

Within a relationship, one is often the other's opposite. Each person complements the other, and together the two people are in harmony. The problem with our popular culture is that many people see the marriage union or an intimate relationship made up of two halves that complete each other to become one whole. Not only does this imply one must be or behave in a certain way that fits the perfect picture, it also means that neither one of the two parts is complete on its own. In the Hollywood movie *Jerry Maguire*, Jerry (played by Tom Cruise) says to Dorothy (Renee Zellweger) "You complete me" in his attempt to win her back, and all the women in the scene say "oh". It seems so romantic for a moment, but the concept of needing to be completed by someone else is actually very debilitating.

In this book, the concepts apply equally to same-sex relationships. One partner will often bring in more masculine energy and the other more feminine energy. But when they are both developed, there's a wholeness and harmony to be felt within oneself.

A mature Hera understands the power of union but at the same time, she is fully aware of her own unique strength and authority. The partnership is her leverage, not her only asset. Hera can do well in any profession she chooses, but once she gets married, she has a tendency to shift her focus on supporting her husband or family.

Many Heras are extroverted and sensate by nature, meaning that they are outwardly oriented. Hera has a strong sense what is happening around her. Hera women tend to pay attention to their appearance and to symbols of culture that carry meaning. So inside there is the drive to become a wife, which is truly a pressure from within, but because she is extroverted she may fail to see the true character of the man she is drawn to, and will fantasize about them together as a power couple or well-suited pair.

## Relationships with Hera

Hera is often drawn to a man that the culture sees as a potential Zeus, someone who is ambitious, energetic and charming. He is admired, or may be a leader among his peers and he is someone who is expected to make a name for himself or achieve something great. Hera is attracted to these promising masculine qualities. Often she has sensed some vulnerability in him, or he may have gotten close and opened up to her. There is an emotional hook for seemingly strong and successful men to show her their sensitive sides.

If a Hera marries the wrong man or if the marriage doesn't work out, she will be devastated. We know that once the honeymoon was over, Zeus went off to make many more conquests, have more children and extend his dynasty further and further. Each time Hera found out about an affair, she became enraged and wounded. In the myths, she had no mercy for the women, who were after all seduced by Zeus, and she was driven to punish them and punish their children. The myths certainly detail some extreme retribution. What this means in reality is that sometimes Hera the archetype has such a grip on a woman's psyche and it is hard for her to let go and to forgive.

Hera may have divorced her former husband, he may even have remarried or started a new family. But if the grip of the archetype is very strong, or if Hera is unwilling to move on, the topic of her former husband may come up a lot in her conversations, as she may retain her hurt from the divorce for many years. However, some Hera women are able to move past that phase and understand that they never really needed a husband to complete them. Certainly time is needed for Hera to grieve and heal first.

Hera is queenly, she doesn't necessarily want people to see her suffer, to feel pity or sorrow for her. She doesn't want to feel vulnerable and weak. That said, growth often comes after a difficult time that stretches our capacity to love. After a breakdown, there is a breakthrough. As a Hera emerges from her dark nights of the soul, she will likely grow into other archetypes and develop other parts of herself. She will see that higher purposes await her, that there are deeper and further meanings for her to experience in life. If she considers marriage again, she will most likely choose someone whose character and fidelity are more suited to her and who also honours the sacred bond of marriage.

## Hera mother and her children

Women who have Hera as the dominant archetype are committed to being a wife. Once she marries she takes on the role of arranging the social life, family visits, holidays and so on for the family. She will make sure everything is presentable, such as the children or the home, and she maintains an immaculate appearance in public.

At home, if she must choose to side with her husband or her children, she will likely go with her husband to please him, and tell the children to respect their father's wishes. This is why many children of Hera may have problems with their mothers, because they are not allowed to go against their father. For example, if a daughter wants to go out with a boy or a son wants to travel in his gap year, but the father is stubborn and difficult and refuses to approve it, Hera is unlikely to intervene on behalf of her children. This type of situation can lead to a distance between parents and children as open communication or fairness isn't firmly established in the family.

Although Hera may side with the father due to her allegiance to her husband, she may still get into disagreements or fights with him, as she is after all a strong woman. Not all Hera women marry a Zeus who is unfaithful and narcissistic, but if they do, and in scenarios where there is an extramarital affair, the children may become aware of it or even witness arguments between their parents. This may impact on their view of relationships, marriage and parenthood. Therefore, Hera's influence on her children can be very powerful. How she matures or evolves into a grown and wise woman can greatly affect her relationships with her children.

If Hera is the natural dominant archetype in a daughter, she is likely to talk about her dream wedding and how she would like to meet "the one" in her life. There are fewer young Hera girls around us these days, but at a certain point in life, this archetype may surface and be energised. Suddenly, finding true love and getting married becomes an important priority, and so a Hera is activated.

## What can we learn from Hera

There are two sides to Hera, the light side is the regal, queenly, powerful one, with clear boundaries, action orientation and the respect of those around her. The shadow side is the angry, vindictive, temperamental woman, which is often portrayed by the myths in her fights with Zeus. The other aspects that are rarely mentioned are her charisma, charm and intellectual capacity as Queen. There is a saying that behind every highly successful man, there is always an equally incredible woman. Sometimes it is this woman who has the ear of a powerful man who speaks the truth when no one else will dare. Or she is the one who whispers strategy or wisdom into his ears when no one else has the capacity. That is Hera. For every great US president, there has been a notable first lady. Think about Eleanor Roosevelt or Jackie Kennedy. They are images of a modern and powerful Hera. Jackie Kennedy once said that her greatest service to the United States while she lived in the White House was to take care of John F. Kennedy. We should never underestimate the importance of the function of a supportive, nurturing, compassionate and loving wife.

Hera's strengths are loyalty and devotion, and there are many marriages that have survived through crises of infidelity, health problems, financial issues and other mishaps because of the capacity and determination of Hera. She is the woman intent on living through difficult times and she usually comes through.

When we make a deep connection and it is broken, hurt, or lost, there is often a sense of disillusionment, disappointment, anger, pain and grief that can feel like the breaking of our hearts.

If the husband who loves Hera sees the pain he has caused and develops his own capacity for empathy, it's possible to repair the marriage and grow back together. Hera must learn more autonomy, which means developing other goddess archetypes and extending her life beyond her husband. But if Hera is the archetype that is strongest in a woman, she will want to stay and see it through. Usually, if the relationships survives, it's because of her.

We see the vulnerabilities and struggles in the relationships of the goddesses such as Demeter, Persephone and Hera, and their growth journey is usually through life experiences and relationships. The lessons from their relationships become their focus, not external material achievements. These 'relationship-oriented' goddesses are more inward focused compared to the more outward goals-focused goddesses like Athena or Artemis. When Hera emerges from her challenging times, she will be more humble and teachable, and more in touch with her pain and desire.

## Ways to grow beyond

Archetypes are useful because people commonly fit into certain patterns which help us understand them, and our relationships with them. However, people are more complex than archetypes, because people can change and grow. We can learn from our actions and their consequences, and we can choose to do things differently when similar situations arise. We can also adapt and learn from different archetypes as we grow. Although we cannot change our stories in the past, we can most certainly change our thoughts and actions and create a different story for our future.

Not all Hera women will necessary go through a break up or crisis with their husbands. But there will always be challenges in a long-term relationship no matter how complementary two people are. Conflict can enable two individuals to smooth out their rough edges. It is part of their soul growth. The heart of the matter is that Hera needs to remind herself that being a wife is only part of her identity, she is so much more. She needs to see her own worth, her individuality and stand in her own power. Sometimes emotions get the better of us and we forget who we really are, and only remember how we feel in the moment.

If a Hera refuses to go through the doors of transformation and remains in the same dysfunctional dynamic in which she always puts her husband first, she will become codependent. Codependence cuts across many different categories and different depths and widths. They tend to give themselves away, and will insist on doing what the other person wants instead of what she wants. Codependence also means that she doesn't know where and how to apply love to herself. Demeter is another archetype that has a codependent tendency, a tendency to put someone else first, like her children.

If a Hera has to go through a radical and challenging situation, for example a divorce, a serious illness in the family or a financial crisis, when she finally returns from her dark night of the soul, she will be totally transformed. Think of the symbolic meaning of the resurrection of the phoenix, which rises from the ashes that fire has purified. The past has been released. She will be reborn as an even more beautiful and powerful creature. She will see things from a new perspective that can enrich her life.

# Self-care for Hera

## Aromatherapy

Hera is confident, poised and queenly. She is loyal, determined and can be forceful when she does not feel things are right. Hera's blend should include rose otto and rose absolute along with sandalwood or cedarwood oil. It would not hurt to balance this with a dash of bergamot or a zesty sharp citrus oil.

*For more information on Aromatherapy and the Goddesses, please refer to Appendix 1.*

## Well-being practices

The most important practice for a Hera is to find out what really matters in her heart. If she lets go of her role as a wife, who is she?

- Journaling – to reflect on who is she and what is truly important for her.
- Meditation – to practice stillness and go inward.
- Yoga – to connect and become more aware of her body.

- Solitude – to really get to know her inner voice.
- Nature – a great way to connect to her soul.

## ❝ Note-to-self:

*A woman is like a tea bag. You can't tell how strong she is until you put her in hot water.*
*– Eleanor Roosevelt*

*Sometimes letting things go is an act of far greater power than defending or hanging on.*
*– Eckhart Tolle* ❞

## Self-reflective questions

You may like to answer these self-reflective questions as you read through this book or schedule some quiet time in your week to focus on going within. It may be a nice way to prepare yourself by doing a 10 to 15-minute meditation before writing down your thoughts. There are no rules; whichever ways can help you to connect with your inner self will be beneficial to you.

- Would you say that Hera is a major or minor archetype in you?
- Did/do you feel pressure to get married?
- What would it mean to you if married? What would it mean to you if you did not?
- What about your mother? Was she a Hera wife whose husband was her priority?

- In what ways was she maternal or not?
- If you have had a series of relationships that did not last, would more or less Hera have made a difference?
- Do you put the needs of your husband before your own?

Positive Affirmation

*I am empowered.*

# APHRODITE

*Goddess of Beauty and Love*

Archetype: Alchemist and Transformer

*Muse, speak to me of the works of Aphrodite,*
*the golden one, the Cyprian,*
*the one who awakens sweet longing in the gods*
*and subdues the race of human beings*
*and the birds that fly through the air*
*and all the wild beasts and the many creatures*
*the dry land feeds, the sea nourishes.*
*all these love what she brings to pass,*
*the Cytherean in her lovely crown.*
**– Hymn to Aphrodite**[23], *The Homeric Hymns*

## WHO IS APHRODITE?

One of the most portrayed goddesses in our contemporary culture. Aphrodite's image of beauty and romantic love is deeply embedded in our collective psyche. The word "aphro" means foam, so her name literally translates as "she who comes from the foam." The Romans knew Aphrodite as Venus. As we learned from the myth of Athena in Chapter 3, Cronus castrated Uranus and threw his man-parts into the sea and from this Aphrodite arose. As one would expect, the myth emphasizes her connection to sexuality and femininity. Ocean has long been associated with the divine feminine. Born of sea foam and impregnated by heaven, Aphrodite floated ashore on the islands near Greece, where she was greeted by the lovely maidens called the Three Graces, who dressed the goddess in attire worthy of her beauty and who became her constant companions. The famous painting "*The Birth of Venus*" by Sandro Botticelli has depicted this myth.

It is well known that this goddess is associated with beauty, love, sensuality, sexuality, romance and passion. These are certainly her attributes, but not all of them. In fact, they all point to a deep and powerful ability, the ability to transform oneself and others. Aphrodite's birth, was a transformation of the sea, which represents feminine energy. We know an Aphrodite when we meet one, she may or may not possess physical beauty, as the world defines it, but she always has a magnetism about her. It is not always an attraction to her sexuality, as one might assume, but rather the connection that she makes you feel. She is very present and engaged in the conversations you have together, she listens and she sees you, she is with you. The world may seem to have disappeared around you but you are charmed by the Aphrodite energy. This feeling is almost addictive.

Aphrodite likes beautiful things, like clothes and jewellery, but she is very interested in people so she doesn't come across as totally obsessed with her appearance. When she meets someone, she is more focused on that person than on herself. But of course she is attractive in her own right.

The myths of Aphrodite tell us a lot about her, but often we need to go deeper to truly understand the power of this goddess. The interesting part of Aphrodite is her autonomy in the midst of patriarchal culture. In most cases, the major gods can have their way with any mortal woman, any nymph or any goddess, except the virgin goddesses Athena and Artemis. But not Aphrodite, she is in the unique position of being desired by all the gods, so she can choose amongst them. She chooses to marry Hephaestus, the God of the Forge. Despite his imperfection (he has a clubfoot), he is the creator of beautiful things such as jewellery, ornaments, crafts and other hand-made adornments. Aphrodite also has very notable liaisons with Ares, the God of War, Hermes, the Messenger God, and she also falls in love with Adonis, whom we learned about the love triangle between Aphrodite, Adonis and Persephone in Chapter 6.

The archetypal influence of Aphrodite may lead a woman to fall in love, frequently, but it doesn't necessarily mean this archetype will always lead women into extramarital affairs. It is a personal choice, just because she has such a mesmerizing power over people, doesn't mean Aphrodite will always use it irresponsibly. She may also fall in love with creative projects or passionate pursuits and meaningful causes.

The best things about Aphrodite are her deep appreciation of beauty and her sense of gratitude that can go with reverence or awe. Aphrodite has a special power, which people around her feel strongly.

I watched an Aphrodite in action once. She was leading a spiritual and inspirational weekend seminar, and that day, the topic was romantic love. During the Q&A session, a young woman from the audience asked a question about why she had so many relationships with men, but they all failed. I watched the Aphrodite teacher coaching the young Aphrodite student. They were both so present and honest in that conversation, it was as if time had stopped. The young woman eventually revealed that she had not been very compassionate or considerate with men's emotions. The teacher simply said, "stop toying with their emotions. Start to wear the big girl pants and be serious. Be a woman and go deep in love". It was a very powerful moment. We knew something was going to change for the young woman, who was in tears. We heard the teacher's love stories all weekend. We knew she had been there herself, that those were her tears too. It was a poignant moment watching a mature Aphrodite leading a young Aphrodite towards transformation into a woman.

## Archetype of an Alchemist and Transformer

In Greek mythology, Aphrodite has an incredible presence, causing mortals and deities (with the exception of the virgin goddesses) to fall in love and conceive new life. She inspires poetry and persuasive speech, and she symbolizes the transformative and creative power of love.

For Aphrodite, relationships are important, but not necessarily as long-term commitments to other people. Aphrodite seeks to consummate relationships and generate new life. This archetype may be expressed through physical relationships or through creative projects.

We experience the alchemy of Aphrodite when we feel drawn toward another person and fall in love; we feel it when we are touched by her power of transformation and creativity; we experience her power when we appreciate the capacity we have to love to the fullest, and then make room for more. She is the spark and the catalyst of a transcendental experience. When she is understood correctly, she is the most transformative archetype.

When Aphrodite influences a relationship, her effect is not limited to the romantic or sexual side of things alone. She also represents platonic love, soul connection, deep friendship, rapport, and empathic understanding, as all these are expressions of love. Whenever growth is generated, a vision supported, potential developed, a spark of creativity encouraged, these are all part of Aphrodite's influence.

Since an Aphrodite woman is often very attractive, feminine in her appearance and surrounded by many suitors, she may seem similar to a Persephone woman. However, if we look closer, we can see the difference

between these two archetypes. First, Aphrodite is more extroverted and Persephone more introverted. They can both be vulnerable when they are young and innocent but as they mature and grow older, it becomes clear that Persephone is inwardly directed. Persephone is often very intuitive, she is interested in spirituality and psychology, and she has a strong ability to understand symbology and the deeper meanings of things. Aphrodite is more drawn to creative endeavors and transformative experiences. Archetypes are not always clear-cut and simple, and we can have more than one archetype working within us, such as both Aphrodite and Persephone. However, usually one is more dominant at any given time.

When Aphrodite is ascendant, a woman is not overly interested in invisible things. She's interested in tangible things that she can see, touch, hear or feel. Her eyes will be drawn to things that are aesthetically pleasing, or things that have the raw potential to be beautiful. She is someone who loves fine wine and food, good music and things that are lovely to touch. Persephone doesn't share these interests as she grows older. But it can be confusing, because women shift between archetypes throughout their lives. Women can be late bloomers, who fully develop the attributes of their strongest archetype, and really own them, only when they grow older.

## Myth of Aphrodite

We have learned about Aphrodite's birth and her dispute with Persephone over Adonis, but there is another myth worth mentioning here as it tells us about the effect of Aphrodite. The 'Pygmalion Effect' originates from the myth of Pygmalion. It's been well-researched that if working with a teacher, psychotherapist, or anyone who is really drawing out your potential can lead you to fulfilling or expressing that potential more fully. The Pygmalion Effect describes the phenomenon in which higher expectations lead to an increase in performance.

Pygmalion was a Cypriot sculptor and he created a beautiful statue of a woman in ivory. He worked with his hands, chiseled her features and finished them with care. When she was complete, he kept her in a special room and he would come and gaze at her. He found the statue was incredibly beautiful and he fell in love with it. However his family, of course, expected him to marry a real woman. So he pleaded with Aphrodite to find him a woman as lovely as his statue. He prayed and made offerings at Aphrodite's altar. When he returned home from these prayers one day, he kissed his ivory statue, and found that its lips felt warm. He kissed it again, and found that the ivory had lost its hardness. Aphrodite had granted Pygmalion's wish. He married the ivory sculpture that had become a woman, and named her Galatee with Aphrodite's blessing. This myth symbolizes the power of love, and the way it can transform a lifeless statue into a living being of flesh and blood. Aphrodite is an alchemist and transformer. She can have an amazing effect on people by helping them to realise and then actualize their dreams and potential.

# Careers for Aphrodite

Since Aphrodite is naturally drawn to artistic expressions and tactile experiences, she thrives working in design, fine arts, crafts, creative arts, fashion, beauty, performance arts or anything that allows for creativity. She needs stimulation and change. The best thing about working in creative professions is the constant supply of new projects, nothing gets stuck in a rut. Even if there are repetitions, such as performing in a theatre play, each performance can elicit a new experience in the actor and the audience.

If an Aphrodite doesn't work in the creative professions, she may have hobbies or interests that are related to creativity, beauty and pleasure.

Aphrodite women are also frequently drawn to healing and therapeutic work. An Aphrodite may be a life coach, trainer, teacher, psychotherapist, counsellor, energy healer or massage therapist. She has an ability to really get to know and understand people, and she is totally immersed in what she does. Sometimes she may even find it hard to withdraw herself from her work. However, when she does detach or another interesting project comes into her life, she will once again fully dive into the new project and easily let go of the old.

# Aphrodite Daughter and Mother

An Aphrodite little girl is usually extroverted and genuinely interested in people. Often she is a real charmer and very pretty. She can easily become the center of attention and people intuitively know she is going to be in trouble with the boys when she grows up. She is often aware there is something special about her and that she can get her way with things. She likes beautiful things and she has a quality of presence about her. For the Aphrodite girl, it is about being right here, right now. She doesn't cry about yesterday or worry about tomorrow. She is very present in the current moment.

When she starts to grow into a woman's body in puberty, she becomes initiated from a girl to a young woman. Often she is popular with the people around her. She can become aware of boys quite young and enjoys the fact that they are attracted to her. This is where trouble may arise, when she is not yet a woman, but she is curious about her body and how she feels when she interacts with a boy. Depending on her family upbringing and religious background, she may receive valuable guidance and wisdom so that she knows what to be careful about in her interactions with the boys.

Sexuality is a powerful force, and when it is overemphasized, it becomes the major expression of who Aphrodite is, even though she is much more than just sexuality. She needs to be aware of this power and how to appropriately relate to another person with her sexuality.

If Aphrodite is your mother, the feeling she gives you when she focuses on you can be very seductive. You may recall how wonderful it was if you were her firstborn when you had all her attention But it can feel very empty when she is gone. In general, she draws people towards her and it feels great to be around her and with her.

# Relationships with Aphrodite

Aphrodite is beautiful, attractive, sensual and often finds herself in romantic relationships. Intercourse is synonymous with communication or communion, consummation may speak of an urge toward completion or perfection, union means to join together as one, but to know is to actually understand another person. The desire to know and be known is what Aphrodite generates. This is the force that truly drives her and the reason she is known for having many romantic relationships and falling easily in love. Now the trouble is, people fall in love with Aphrodite easily too, but they may not find it easy to stop, even if the relationship has ended and Aphrodite has already moved on. She may also give people a wrong impression when she seems so interested in who they are and what they do. Aphrodite may simply be genuinely drawn to the person or their work, without any romantic implications. However, because of her magnetism, she may be misinterpreted and hence people find her misleading. It can also be the case that people are just drawn to her, no matter whether or not she is reciprocating.

## What can we learn from Aphrodite

Many goddesses in the Greek mythologies are powerful yet vulnerable, some of them are betrayed, ignored or even abducted in their myths. They suffer through their relationships or personal journeys. But not Aphrodite. In her myths, she is a revered goddess because she picks and chooses who she will engage in relationship and then she allows herself to be involved. There is a phase in which Aphrodite is affected by the attraction, such as the beauty she sees in the other person. This is what some call an Aphrodite consciousness, it means that she sees through the eyes of compassion and love, and hence recognizes the true potential and beauty in a person. For her, it is never about possessing but appreciating what she sees. When she is drawn to the beauty she goes from attraction to union or impregnation of a new life. This does not always lead to giving birth to children literally, it can be a creative project, a business venture or a new life together as a couple.

Jung described the way an archetype like Aphrodite affects another person as chemical, and later it was much clearer that he was using the word 'alchemy'. He considered the process to be like a chemical reaction in which one substance is affected by the other, and both are changed. This is Aphrodite's alchemical effect, the power to transform others and to be transformed herself at the same time. In each relationship, creative endeavour or passionate pursuit, an Aphrodite always learns something or gains a valuable experience. She is willing and open to change, she is not fixated on anything to stay in a certain way. She perpetuates growth in herself and others.

The power of an Aphrodite alchemy, which can be non-sexual, is the mutuality, magnetic and soulful attraction. It can be as simple as a conversation that has a divine eternal quality. This is why Aphrodite is such an attractive archetype. In the glow of total Aphrodite focus, the other person feels he or she is seen as beautiful, as interesting and as fascinating. There is a sense of the timeless and the limitless, which is the Aphrodite influence.

## Ways to grow beyond

The fact that an Aphrodite can become totally immersed in a relationship or a work project is a gift, but it can also be a problem. It will be helpful to develop some aspects of Athena, to be practical, rational and strategic as these qualities will be complementary to Aphrodite's tendency to lose time and her sense of responsibility as she becomes mesmerized in her current pursuit. Also if an Aphrodite goes from one project to another, and devotes all her energy to each one, her energy will eventually run out. If she jumps from one relationship to another, she also may miss out on the time and opportunity to reflect and grow. Sometimes the best thinking we have about relationships is when we are not in one.

Athena is also a great ally for Aphrodite because Athena is always sensible and responsible. Aphrodite loves beautiful things, such as art, clothes and jewellery. She can fall in love with a lot of different tangible things and she has a strong urge to possess them, which may lead to rash financial decisions.

An Aphrodite woman, who is attractive, extroverted and charismatic, needs to be aware of her power and what she can do to other people. In some cases she needs to be able to define her intentions, so the other person does not assume there is sexual attraction on her side.

Whether Aphrodite is a threat to other women, depends on her ethical boundaries. If she doesn't respect or honour other women and intentionally seduces married men, she is simply unkind and inappropriate. But not all Aphrodites are like that, they can be ethical and careful handling their effect on others. Aphrodite needs to have a strong sense of boundaries, transparency and responsibility.

An Aphrodite may have a tendency to throw herself into a relationship and be consumed with it for its duration. But when she decides it's finished, it is over. Even though she may still have feelings for the other person, she may end the relationship for other reasons. The other person may find it hard to accept the change in her interest or to transition out of the relationship. It is important for an Aphrodite to treat these break ups with tenderness and compassion. She is someone we hear saying "I love you, but I am just not in love with you". She does fall in love each time, but it doesn't last. While she is able to move on, the other person may not be. As Confucius teaches us, "don't do unto others what you don't want others to do unto you." For an Aphrodite to grow beyond her archetypal influence, she needs to learn how to treat herself and others with love, no matter if it is at the beginning of a relationship or the end of it. It may take several serious relationships or even marriages before she can grow beyond this tendency, and be able to appreciate qualities that last rather than attractions that fade. With that ability, she will be able to stay in a relationship for a long time, which provides an opportunity for another level of soul growth.

# Self-Care for Aphrodite

## Aromatherapy

Aphrodite is fully present and radiant. She enjoys pleasure and beauty in life. A rich floral, spicy-sweet blend would be perfect for Aphrodite. Blend some jasmine absolute and ylang ylang together along with lots of benzoin, sweet orange and some coriander seed.

*For more information on Aromatherapy and the Goddesses, please refer to Appendix 1.

## Well-being practices

The key thing for Aphrodite is to learn how to fall in love with herself, to go within, to know she has all she needs internally and she does not need external influences or stimulations all the time.

- Yoga – to calm the mind and benefit many other body systems.
- Meditation – to practice stillness and to go inward.
- Dancing – to express desires and emotions through physical movement and creativity.

- ꕤ Journaling – helpful to self-reflect on your own emotions and relationships with others.

##  NOTE-TO-SELF:

*To love oneself is the beginning of a lifelong romance.*
– Oscar Wilde

*There is no charm equal to tenderness of heart.*
– Jane Austen

## Self-reflective questions

You may like to answer these self-reflective questions as you read through this book or schedule some quiet time in your week to focus on going within. It may be a nice way to prepare yourself by doing a 10 to 15-minute meditation before writing down your thoughts. There are no rules; whichever ways can help you to connect with your inner self will be beneficial to you.

- ꕤ Recall your experiences of falling in love and falling out of love. How did you fall out of love? Perhaps there was an archetypal shift, what happened?
- ꕤ Think of the phrase "Beauty is in the eye of the beholder". Recall how you personally know this truth.
- ꕤ Think about beauty being "skin deep" or "soul deep", and what activates Aphrodite attractions in you, what qualities in another person are you most attracted to now?

- Do you have a relationship that is purely platonic? What do you learn from it?
- The Pygmalion Effect is the ability to see the potential in another person and draw it out, which can help the other person realize and actualize his/her dreams or goals. Do you have any experience of the Pygmalion Effect? What wisdom have you gained?

## Positive Affirmation

*I am love.*

# EMERGING AS A GODDESS

## *Discovering Your Destiny*

*The Goddess doesn't act on events from the outside;
she emerges from deep within us.*
– *A Woman's Worth,* **Marianne Williamson**

## FINDING AND LIVING YOUR PERSONAL MYTH

We have read the myths of the six goddess archetypes in the last few chapters, so the next question is, how do they relate to us personally? Some of them are easily recognizable, for example the myth about Persephone. Many of us can identify a sudden emotional crisis in our lives and remember how our world changed after that. With some of the myths we simply resonate with the story, almost as a precautionary tale.

Mythological images are the images by which the conscious is put in touch with the unconscious. They are universal and metaphoric. We find ourselves drawn to certain myths or real-life stories when they really strike a chord. It is because deep down we know there is wisdom and meaning for us to learn there. Myths come from our psyche and they talk to our psyche. When you don't have mythological images or when your consciousness rejects them for some reason, you are out of touch with your own deepest part.

Carl Jung talked about finding and living personal myths in his autobiographical work *Memories, Dreams and Reflections*. He says "it struck me what it means to live with a myth and what it means to live without one.[24]" If you live by myths that guide you, you are aware of what life lessons you are going through or what transformation you are seeking. There is a sense of clarity and purpose in life. At heart, you know what really matters and what you want to accomplish in life.

In his highly acclaimed book *Man's Search For Meaning*, the Austrian psychiatrist and Holocaust survivor Viktor Frankl wrote about how important it is to identify a purpose in life and to feel positively about it. In his case, it may have even been the difference between life and death during his first-hand experience as a prisoner in the Auschwitz concentration camp.

For most of us, the circumstances are less extreme but if we make the effort to pay attention to the wisdom of the myths that draw us and if we reflect on what calls us, our life will be dramatically different. We cannot stay dormant when we are awake. We have a guiding light within us. We have a sense of the right step to take or right change to make. The wisdom of myth makes it harder for us to stay where we are when we are not happy or at peace.

This is essentially what Joseph Campbell meant by his famous statement "follow your bliss". Find out what makes your heart sing and what makes you happy, and then do it. It can be a hobby or a profession or a cause, there are no restrictions on what can or cannot be your bliss. Sir Ken Robinson, a world renowned education advisor wrote about "the element" in two of his books, which refers to the experience of personal talent meeting personal passion, and how this can lead us to our most inspired self and to reach the highest level of achievement. That is another way to look at bliss, to be in your element. Personally I see it as what makes me feel excited to start my day, what uplifts me when I have a bad day, what makes my heart warm and what keeps me going even if I am tired or have doubts.

Since the day I decided to look deeper in life and started paying attention to divine synchronicity, or simply how the universe works, I have been humbled and awed many times. It could be meeting a person by chance that changed my life, or watching the birth of my baby and the way she grows every day. There is something greater than ourselves. There is an invisible yet powerfully intelligent energy that moves through us. The same energy that programs the flower bud to become a rose and the embryo to become a baby.

You don't need to force it to happen, in fact, you shouldn't and couldn't. You want to allow it and flow with it. You can however, prepare yourself to be ready for something grand to happen in your life. Following the bliss is not the same as following the roses. Life isn't always a walk in the park. Even if you have found your element and are given great opportunities, there will be challenges and surprises. It is about how you respond, instead of react, and whether or not you are willing to learn and to grow. You can make conscious decisions and take willful steps towards your own transformation, to transcend into the greatest version of yourself, the one you are meant to be.

## Transactional vs Transcendental Thinking

A lot of things happening in the world relate to the praise and practice of transactional thinking. The "what do I want to get out of this?" kind of thinking. It may be about a job or relationship or simply a meeting. There is nothing wrong about having a clear objective or a goal, but confining your focus to an individual transactional outcome will be short sighted at best and missing the grand picture at worst.

The idea of transcendental thinking means going beyond and above common or ordinary experience. Transactional thinking will go like this "I want this relationship to yield a marriage, a husband who has a good job and a promised secure future". We all want a great relationship, but wouldn't it be better to say "I feel attracted to this man, I am yet to find out where it will lead us, but I am open to any lessons and experiences that this relationship may bring me. I am here for love and a deeper connection that will last." Now you have opened the gate to endless possibilities in your mind. This is a far more magnetic and expansive energy than restrictive thinking.

In truth, we all want our lives to be above and beyond the ordinary. It is our birthright to shine. As described in *A Course In Miracles*, it is not humble but arrogant to think God would give us a function that we cannot fulfill. Just think about how much it would change your perspective in life if you thought you were meant to shine.

So now we know it is probably a good idea to play a *bigger* game in life, to go above and beyond our transactional or limited thinking. But deep transformation often originates from our unconscious, so how do we recognize the trigger of transformation? And how do we prepare for all the challenges and changes that will come along with it?

## What is a hero/heroine journey?

The turning point or trigger of transformation is often the moment when you decide to say no to something that you can no longer tolerate or refuse to accept. In myths, it may be the scenario of a maiden refusing her suitors or a hero opposing the tyranny of a king.

Joseph Campbell defines a Hero Journey as a soul adventure. In mythology, the outer journey may be about saving a loved one or finding an elixir. In the movie *Lord of The Rings*, it was about destroying the One Ring and hence eliminating the Dark Lord Sauron. The first *Star Wars* movie, *A New Hope*, centers on the mission to rescue the Princess Leia, help the Rebel Alliance and restore freedom and justice in the Galaxy. These are all Hero Journey examples where the basic story involves leaving your ordinary life and going into the realm of adventure, then coming to some kind of symbolically rendered realization and finally returning to the field of normal life. However, this normal life is forever changed by the adventure. This is because in order to reach the outer designation, to fulfill the external mission, one must have undergone an internal transformation.

This transformation shapes the Hero/Heroine into the person he or she needed to be in order to succeed. Some people may feel uneasy identifying with the word "hero" or "heroine", wondering what qualifies one to be

a hero. However even if you are not a self-proclaimed hero, you become one as soon as you answer the call, the inner calling asking you to do what is right for yourself or for others. Frodo doesn't look particularly heroic when we first meet him in the *Lord of the Rings*. A hero is never born, but only *becomes* one through his or her experiences. In this book I use the term Heroine Journey instead of Hero Journey because I am a woman and many of my examples have come from my personal experience. However, there is no distinction between the two here. Both a hero and a heroine are basically the protagonist of the journey. Also, the elements and stages in this book are based on my own interpretation, observations and personal experiences regarding the Hero/Heroine Journey. For a more detailed study on the Hero Journey from the author who named it, the best reference will be Joseph Campbell's book, *The Hero With A Thousand Faces*.

## STAGE 1: THE CALL TO ADVENTURE

In life, knowing it or not, we have all gone through at least one Heroine Journey and possibly many more. Some are triggered by biological changes and some are due to emotional or spiritual experiences. For example motherhood, puberty, menopause, leaving a job, starting a business, ending a relationship or starting a new one, all these are opportunities and invitations for a Heroine Journey to begin. You can either be thrown into it or you can walk intentionally in. However, sometimes the call to adventure can be subtle or unconscious. There is a stirring in you towards change, but you are not quite sure what it is, or maybe you know what it is, but you are not sure if you are ready for it. Many of us had this experience. For me, I had a feeling that I wanted to write a book about transformation for women, but I never talked about it. That is very atypical of me, as I normally love to bounce ideas off people. Then one day I was discussing some current projects with my mentor, and he said "Maybe you should write a book about it". As soon as he said it, I knew it was officially a call to adventure. Not only did he suggest it, but he has been instrumental in bringing this book to life from that moment on.

By the time he suggested writing a book, I had already studied a lot of material related to this topic over many years, and I had been using it in my seminars and coaching. The Heroine Journey is always "dangerous" in a sense that you are moving out of the familiar sphere of your community or comfort zone. I was confident in communicating what I've learned to my seminar audiences and applying the concepts in real-life situations. But I was not entirely confident about writing a book. This was partly because I am not a native speaker, English is my second language. I also felt I needed to make sure that the book is relatable, useful and enjoyable for readers. None of these skills are familiar or easy. So I didn't really commit to the idea until my mentor suggested it to me. In myths, this stage is represented as leaving the known and entering the unknown. The soul adventure invokes something we didn't know we had within us, and so we refuse the adventure at first, because we resist change and we don't trust that we have the potential already in us.

When I started this book, I knew there were a lot of rich materials in mythology, psychology and spirituality that I wanted to share. I knew at the deepest level that they are all connected, but I wasn't sure I would be able to put them all together in a meaningful and practical way. I didn't want to write a book that was merely composed of intellectual concepts, I wanted it to be truly helpful for women or men to understand themselves, their relationships with one another and to become better versions of who they already are. I had doubts about whether I could do all that, let alone take this book to the market and be discovered. But my faith won over my doubts.

And I know clearly in my heart that this book project is not about me. Not at all. I need to transcend from fear to love. If there is a reason for this to happen, I need to become the conduit not the clog. Instead of worrying about whether I can do it or what people may think of me, I need to focus on how I can be most helpful, how I may serve a greater purpose. Someone said "worrying is like praying for the worst outcome." So whenever the dark clouds creep in, and they do, I remind myself it is good to be in the unknown, because that is where we cross the threshold into our Heroine Journey to go through our trials and learn our lessons. I have learned that illuminations happen when we just keep moving along this journey.

## Stage 2: Initiation and right to passage

When we decide on taking the Heroine Journey, something miraculous happens. Some call it Supernatural Aid. A teacher or coach or mentor or an inspirational figure comes into your life. He/she may not be what you expected, but someone will come along and illuminate your path. It could be a personal encounter, or it can happen through a book or podcast or a video. It is about receiving what you need to help you with your upcoming trials.

When you embark on your adventure, entering the world of the unknown and extraordinary, you will meet helpers as well as challengers. That is when the tests or trials happen. There are four kind of trials in Campbell's Hero Journey. We see them all the time in myths and in movie plot lines. Not all four are necessarily present on your journey but at least one will be required to trigger the transformation. These tests or trials symbolize self-realization, a process of initiation into the mysteries of life. The following is a brief introduction to these trials and how they may show up in our life.

The first one is the sacred marriage, the union between our gendered outward identity and the 'other' within our psyches, for men that is Carl Jung's *anima*, the inner feminine, and for women it is the *animus*, the inner masculine. The challenge is integrating the two energies within one self. It can be presented in myth as the marriage or union between a man and a woman, representing the masculine and feminine natures.

The second one is about atonement with the father. In mythology, there is a notion that mother represents our nature, and father represents our character. Adventures about finding a father translate as finding one's own character or core values. We often see a reconciliation between the father and son/daughter at the end of a movie. It can also represent making amends, to forgive and to be forgiven. The past is released and the future is yet to be formed. From that moment on everything changes.

Another way to look at this powerful word is to break it into at-one-ment. In George Lucas' film, *The Return of the Jedi*, Luke Skywalker risks his life to save the life of his father, Darth Vader, and this is at-one-ment in the extreme. The son saves the father and the father saves the son. However, in my view, atonement as a trial is not restricted to only the concept of father, but is about understanding and applying forgiveness.

The third kind is apotheosis. The climax is reached when you realize that you are what you seek and understand the full scope of yourself. Buddha achieved his enlightenment under a bodhi tree, and it was a self-realization that came from a shift in a physical identification to a spiritual one. Think about the peak moments you have had. Often, you went beyond what you thought you were or capable of. The problem is, we don't access these moments for long enough or often enough. Otherwise we would all be enlightened masters.

The fourth kind of test is magic flight. It is a quick rush through all the obstacles and the seizing of the desired boon, often the Hero/Heroine will be chased by others. In myth, we have the Promethean theft of fire. In the movie *Shawshank Redemption*, Andy Dufresne escaped prison with the warden's lodger as a proof of his corruptions. Think of situations when you abruptly decided to say no to something when everyone expected you to say yes. There may be a line of people after you that try to convince you to change your mind, but all you want to do is to get away from them.

None of the trials are easy or comfortable but they trigger you to look more closely at your life and push you to start to act in a way that is truly aligned with your values and beliefs. In many traditions, ceremonies that mark important transitions in a person's life such as birth, puberty, marriage, the birth of a child and death, are called the rites of passage. With all these tests and trials, you will inevitably grow and gain insight. So the way I see it, you will also earn the right to passage, and your transformation is underway.

# Stage 3: Transformation

All these tests and trials are essential parts of your descent into the deep end of your unconscious, or the abyss, metaphorically. Many myths share the scenario where the Hero/Heroine is swallowed by a monster or whale. Some may call it the dark night of the soul. Now being in the belly of the whale or in the dark means one has no choice but to be totally transformed. What happens when you escape is that you will not be the same person you used to be. It matches what comes after crucifixion, which is resurrection. You will bring out what you went into the abyss to recover, the unrealized and unactualized potential of yourself. You will reintroduce this potential into the world by living it. You will bring this treasure of understanding back and integrate it in your life.

Two problems may happen in this stage, the first problem for some is that we may get stuck in that belly of the whale for far too long, we get used to a damaging situation as the norm, and we grow numb. This can happen, for example, if we are in the deep end of an abusive relationship and we just don't know how to break through this. In another scenario, we start to lose sight of what we thought we were meant to do, we stay in a job that makes us miserable and are unable to leave because of the financial stability it offers. I do not recommend the strategy of "just quit and see what happens" but I am an advocate of planning and taking action to change the situation. You are responsible for your happiness, no one else. Your scenarios may be completely different, but we all need to remember, we cannot stay in the belly of the whale forever, nor stay crucified. We must get off the cross and resurrect.

The second problem is to do with integrating our experience. Sometimes it is not straightforward and often it is work in progress. In both cases, ask for help and support, work with professionals if required. You do not need to do this alone. The only way to get rid of darkness is to turn on the light. Now you must leave the abyss and come back to the known, which is the conscious and the world as we know it. You are forever changed and are now initiated into the mysteries of life. More than that, you got acquainted with the way to begin the mastery of life. This will lead us to the next stage.

## Stage 4: Empowerment

Others have described the stage of The Return as re-emerging in the known and ordinary world. However, contrary to this, I believe this part of the journey is still extraordinary. The reason is that if you have changed, the world you look at will change too. If you have become extraordinary, how can you live in an ordinary world? You won't, because you will see the world differently, you will make it extraordinary for yourself and for others.

All three stages in our soul adventure prepare and lead us to this stage, to inspire us to share our wisdom and shine our light, to allow ourselves the chance to radiate and illuminate. This concept is summed up most elegantly and eloquently by Marianne William, who famously said "Our deepest fear is not that we are inadequate. Our deepest fear is that we are powerful beyond measure. It is our light, not our darkness, that most frightens us." It takes us all these stages to get over our situation-specific fears, learn skills, and gain wisdom and knowledge, so why not use them in the highest possible way? We all have our unique set of talents, gifts, abilities and life experiences to help us do what we are meant to do. So empowerment here means self-empowerment, you give yourself the power to pursue a life of your own design and desire, which is aligned with the deepest meaning and purpose in your life. Each Heroine Journey or soul adventure takes us to another level or place that was unknown to us before. We don't know what else is possible. There is infinite potential in you and mysteries in the world, so allow yourself to be inspired and intrigued. If you view life as such, every transition will bring you wonders instead of worries in life.

## Women's cycle of life

As mentioned earlier, we all go through at least several transitions in life and in fact they are all invitations to a Heroine Journey at different stages. Each journey leads us to encounter an unknown part within us, or external to us. As women, biologically we have some clearly defined transitions. Each woman's menstrual cycle begins when her body is ready to become a woman. This is the stage of the maiden which, like the season of spring, is full of youthful energy and a feeling of all things being possible. Although it may take a woman a lot longer than she would like for her mind to mature in the same way, she is being initiated into womanhood in a rather straightforward manner. Women's rites of passage are built in, as compared with men, whose journeys from boys to men are not as defined by nature, only by mental maturity.

The next stage is summer, when a woman becomes fully grown and becomes a mother. This journey is more complex as she is bringing a new life into the world. She doesn't know how she is going to be as a mother, there is a sense of uncertainty in her psyche. Some women may feel very excited and ready for their impending motherhood, but some may be worried as life is changing and they have little control or experience to prepare them for it. They may also feel they need to put a pause on their career or they may be unsure how to balance the two. That is why these days many women choose to delay motherhood until they feel they are more established in life. There is clear logic behind this decision if a woman wants to make sure she can provide and care for the child in the best way she can. However, there is also a concern that if she waits too long, it may be harder to conceive. My approach is always internal and non-rational, but not irrational. Listen to your inner calling and don't deny an urge if it is what you want, or rush it if you don't feel ready.

Often we think being strong and powerful is about controlling everything. But is that even wise? There are things we simply cannot control, like falling in love. I am an advocate for meditation and self-reflection time. I believe regularly practicing both helps a woman to hear her inner voice and adds clarity to her decisions.

Personally I also had no idea how motherhood would affect my career or if I would be any good at it. All those concerns fell away as soon as my daughter was born. The birthing experience felt nothing short of miraculous, and all the labour pains were literally a rite of passage. The first time we locked eyes, it felt like an instant of holiness. We connected at the deepest level of infinite love. Since then my direction has been clear, it doesn't matter about the past, or whether or not I have enough of Demeter in me, I just need to be the best I can be.

This stage also applies to women who never have biological or adopted children but women who have reached a certain level of maturity and want to bring forth a brain child or a meaningful project into fruition. The mother stage is when we are in full bloom, where growth is visible and vivid. We want to create and bring something meaningful and beautiful to life. We have harnessed some skills and experiences in the world and are the forerunners with endless energy. We are just like a long summer day.

Now in the next stage, we depart from some traditional classifications of women's life stages. You may be familiar with the term the 'triple goddess': the maiden, mother and crone. With longer life expectancy and medical advancement, I believe we need to expand this with a new era for those in middle age and still very active in life. In fact, a woman at this stage may now be the leader of her clan, someone who is very involved in work or personal pursuits. She may hold a senior management position in business or in political life. She may be the leader in a social group. This is the matriarch stage. Elizabeth Davis and Carol Leonard added this stage in their book *The Women's Wheel of Life*. I resonate very much with their description "The Matriarch rekindles the passions and dreams of youth and may pick up broken threads of spiritual pursuits with new intensity and direction." This is the golden age for women, the autumn, and it is time for harvest. We have gained valuable life experience and earned patience and grace.

Some schools of thought use menopause as an indicator of which stage a woman has reached, but for me, biological changes are not the only indicator. I believe a woman who has experienced a lot of challenging events in life, or someone who has a keen reflective nature, will enter their golden age earlier than others. I think both physical and mental maturity need to be taken into account. A woman who is in touch with her inner centre, or spiritual centre will certainly know which season she is in.

Moving to the winter stage of a woman's life, instead of calling older women "crones", I much prefer to call them "wise women". They have entered the age of wisdom, and are no longer at the front of the stage but rather backstage, advising and mentoring younger women in life. Winter signifies a slower pace and a calmer presence. I love winter mornings when the air is crisp and fresh. There is a sense of clarity that no other season can match.

As we move through the four seasons, we know after winter comes spring. Just like watching a grandmother playing with a young granddaughter, the wisdom and love of the aged passes onto youth. We see life continually renew itself if we see ourselves as spirit living a human experience. In *A Course in Miracles*, we are often reminded that birth is not the beginning of life, it is a continuation of life. Death is not the end of life, but it is also a continuation of life. Through the millennia, goddess wisdom lives on, even if the patricahal culture invades much of the old traditional practices, women have always understood the wisdom of collaboration over competition. In our hearts, we always know the important roles we have in life. Through our wombs and words, we will always carry and spread the light and love we hold dear.

# All is One

In many spiritual books or New-Age teachings, we hear the term "All is One" or "We Are All One", and it may be confusing for some or simply sound like a pseudo-spiritual term. My understanding is always based on the distinction between physical and spiritual identification and perception. In a physical sense, I am sitting where I am typing these words, and you are wherever you are reading these words. There is a clear geographical distance and time difference between us. However, if we look at this from a spiritual perspective, our minds are joined, you are reading

what I have written. You are thinking what I am thinking. There is no time and space between us. We are connected at this very instant, this moment. The only time that matters is now, the present moment. The rest can be seen as illusion and doesn't matter or exist at all. So from this spiritual perspective, there is no place where you stop and I start. We are energy or consciousness linked together. We are one. All is One.

Albert Einstein said, "The distinction between the past, present and future is only a stubbornly persistent illusion". This is about the perception of time. If we identify with physical time, we can name the year, month, day and time of day of this moment. But if we think about this from a metaphysical perspective, meaning if we look at the abstract concept of reality and the nature of existence philosophically, only the present moment is real. We cannot change the past or see the future. We cannot touch it, save it or manipulate it. Past and future therefore don't really exist, metaphysically.

Now think about what happens if we shift our physical identification to spiritual identification. That is what enlightenment allows us to do. We shift our perception from physical to spiritual. From there, we understand what oneness really means, and why we should love our neighbours as our brothers, because we are all related, energetically we are one.

What I find really interesting is that until 1956, the de facto motto of the United States was "E pluribus unum" in Latin, which means, "Out of many, one". This motto was adopted by an Act of Congress in 1782. It aligns with the thinking that we are all connected, not separate. The concept puts a new light on what we think about one another and how we relate to one another. It naturally leads us to be kinder to one another, perhaps this is an idea that can also lead us to deeper inner and outer peace.

## Feminine Radiance

We have discussed how women grow with maturity, going through different seasons in life, taking on different Heroine Journeys and transformations, and naturally evolving as a woman individually. Since we are related to one another, we will also evolve together as groups and communities. It is like a ripple effect, the light in me salutes the light in you, and you will pass on this salute too. When a woman finds her voice, she will help others to find theirs. There is a collective movement of awakening happening now. When one goddess emerges, another follows.

We all want to emerge as a goddess, but how do we do it, literally? Perhaps the key here is not about doing, once again, but about being. How we inhabit the space where we stand makes a world of difference, it can lead us to spread our wings or sink into the ground. You can tell when a woman has got "it", a feminine radiance. What "it" really means is open to interpretation, you may find words such as: presence, inner beauty, self-realisation, authenticity, magnetism, mysticism or sensuality appeal to you as qualities of feminine radiance. Like the old saying, all roads lead to Rome, these qualities lead us to a place perhaps more appropriately called Home.

When a woman is "at home with herself", it means she is comfortable in her own skin, she is happy and at peace. What I find is that when women are living with meaning and purpose, they are their most radiant selves, they have found their bliss. So next we will focus on how you can get here.

## From NoWhere to NowHere

Is it about how you look at life? Sure. Is it about looking deeper into the underlying wisdom or silver lining in your experience? Definitely. Our life story is not about what happens to us, the narrative is always about how we got to where we are. If you want to be the captain of your own ship, you must take full responsibility for your thoughts and actions. It is like cause and effect, you need to look at the cause of a problem instead of trying to fix the effect. In the following section, you have the opportunity to look at your personal myth, to see what got you to where you are now, and we will look at some essential elements to set your course towards where you want to go. You may enter the uncharted territory, but you will be guided and you have tools. The following section contains some self-reflective questions that may take time to complete, you can do them all in one sitting, or you can break them up and take some time between answers to reflect. There are no rules, they are questions that aim to help you to gain clarity and courage for what is to come.

## WHO ARE YOU?

After becoming acquainted with the six major Greek goddess archetypes, the chances are you already know which ones are most active in you. Now take some time to relax, maybe do a meditation, or simply close your eyes and take some deep breaths. I want you to go back in time, and start thinking about your life stories like watching a movie in your mind. Spend some time reflecting upon your goddess archetypes. You may like to use the following questions to help you find some clarity.

- Which goddess archetypes describe your natural interests and character as a child? List some of the attributes that align with your natural archetype/s.

- Was your natural archetype encouraged in your family or circumstances? How so? Or did you need to adapt and change? If that is the case, which archetype/s you have activated instead?

- What about now, has another archetype/s started to influence your life? If so, who is it and why? What triggered the change?

- What is the theme of your life right now? Is it about overcoming a challenge? Or is it about an inspiration you would like to develop?

- If there is an archetype you would like to draw on, who is she? Why?

## WHAT IS YOUR PERSONAL MYTH?

Now think about all the major events in your life, some may be pivotal, such as relocating to another country or beginning a new job or something that is simply life changing. Some events may be more emotional in nature, like the break up of a relationship or the loss of a loved one. Some may be celebratory and joyous. We learn our lessons in life through pain or joy, some of them we choose, some of them we don't. But it is always important to think about what we learn from them. I have shared my life stories throughout this book, including some where a seemingly heartbreaking situation has been a blessing in disguise, or at least a nudge to correct my course from a wrong direction. In retrospect, sometimes the worst things that happen in your life can turn out to be the best things. It may even be a divine intervention that stops you detouring from your real life's purpose.

Try to name three significant stories/events of your life. If you can't name three, try at least one.

- What happened?
- What did you learn?
- How did it change your life?
- What came next?

Your life stories become your personal myths, there is always a theme or an overall lesson. There may be multiple themes, specially if you have gone through a lot of significant events in life or as you grow older and more mature. When you examine your life, what naturally happens next is you start to see where you want to head into next. Some may already know this very clearly, but for others, the questions above can bring the clues needed. It may be a good idea to take some time to let the process work in your unconscious. The questions may bring up a lot of emotions and "aha" moments and it often takes time to sink in. You don't have to answer all the questions here in one sitting, you know what works for you best.

## WHAT IS CALLING YOU?

Your Heroine Journey is essentially your soul adventure. A path of personal transformation in which you must first achieve inner change, which is often invisible, in order to reach the visible outer goal.

Your Heroine Journey may start with a longing, something you want to do or change but have never acted upon. You may not know what exactly that longing is, but there is a sense of something being incomplete, or something missing in your life. Then, there is an opportunity. It can present itself as a challenge, to push you to face your fear or to right what is wrong. It can also be an invitation, asking you to leave your comfort zone and take a leap into something far greater than where you are. By now you may already have a good idea about what may set you off on your current Heroine Journey. Regardless, the following questions can help you to articulate your inner calling at this stage:

- Is there something that you tend to think about at night, when you are alone or have time for yourself?

- Are you facing any challenge that you know is a call for change?

- Is there something you feel is missing in your life? What are you doing about it?

- Do you have a longing to express yourself, or to actualize a gift or potential that is deep within you?

- Is there something that really draws your attention, to which you like to devote your free time, or like to read or learn about?

- Do you have a dream that you would like to fulfill? Are you doing something about it?

## Where are you?

After reading about the four seasons of women, you probably have a good idea about you current life stage. Now assume you are on your Heroine Journey and have answered your inner calling to move forward in your life. You may be at various stages, but think about the following:

- Who was/is your magic aid?

*(For example: someone who inspires you through their teaching or life story, or someone who literally steps in and helps you with your situation).*

- What were/are your trials?

Remember there are many kinds of trials, you may have faced one or more of the following examples:

*Sacred Marriage:* the union of feminine and masculine energy within yourself or in a relationship.

*Atonement*: the forgiveness of self and others.

*Apotheosis:* seeing the true essence of who you are and what you seek.

*Magic Flight*: chased or pressured by others after doing something or making a decision that opposes them.

There can also be other kind of tests, such as *temptation* or *confrontation of your fear*.

- How was your descent into the belly of the whale? What was your experience?

- How did you manage to break free or resurrect? If you think you are still in it, what do you need to do to overcome it?

- How was life different afterwards? What changed in your life?

- What are your insights? What have you learned?

- What are you now most grateful for from that experience?

## Heroine Journey Essential Tool Kit

By now you will have gathered a pretty good picture of your personal Heroine Journey, and perhaps even some insights about lessons learned already. We all know life is always a work-in-progress, as we continue to grow and evolve. No matter where you are on your journey or when you are in your life, I find the following elements very helpful to keep me calm, inspired, patient, honest, grounded and at peace. So I would like to share my absolutely essential tools.

## Regular spiritual practice

I highly recommend meditation. There are many types, you may pick whichever one resonates with you. But remember, all meditation is a form of relaxation, but not all relaxation is meditation. If you want to hear your inner calling more clearly or be more in touch with your intuition, this is it. Meditation helps us to train our minds, quiet the outer noise and decrease our levels of stress. You may go to a class or group, use an online program or or get a CD or podcast. The key is being regular and consistent. If you cannot keep a long mediation practice, even 10 to 15 minutes daily will make a big difference. Make it part of your lifestyle. Just like physical exercise, it takes time to build your muscles and strength. It is equally important to maintain them. Meditation is like exercise for your mind, but unlike physical exercise, which aims to keep your body moving well, meditation is about the ability to still your mind. It is never too late to start. Make it an enjoyable practice and you will discover a great tool for life.

**Essential Tool # 1**

*Make meditation a daily practice. Even for just five minutes.*

## Keep it moving

Find a form of physical exercise or movement activity you enjoy and do it often. I love exercises that help me to develop body awareness while working towards building strength and flexibility. Yoga is a great form of exercise that often incorporates a meditation element. I also love dancing with music or walking in nature. Once again, finding something you truly enjoy will guarantee that you will do it often. I often find my best ideas come to me when I am working out, which is another plus.

**Essential Tool # 2**

*Move your body at least three times a week.*

## HOLISTIC HEALTHY LIFESTYLE

It may sound almost cliché but eating a healthy diet, getting adequate sleep and exercising regularly are the cornerstone of living a healthy life. When we have good health, we have more clarity in our minds, we are more ready to respond to challenges or take up an opportunity in an instant. Another great tool I use is aromatherapy, as it can help elevate physical malignancy and it provides emotional and energetic benefits. I always have essential oils with me at work, at home, and when I am travelling. Aromatherapy gives me an instant lift and it is simply a great tool. Use the aromatherapy section in each of the goddess chapters as an easy archetypal reference for you to experience the great benefits of the essential oils in a different way.

**Essential Tool # 3**

*Pick three essential oils that instantly lift your mood or calm your mind and keep them near you.*

## FORGIVENESS – SURRENDER GRATITUDE

It may come as a surprise to many, but often when a business coaching client of mine is asking me why his or her business is so "stuck", I ask them, "Who are you not willing to forgive?". I don't ask this question 100% of the time, but when I do, if my client is willing to explore the answers with me, a breakthrough happens 100% of the time. This is the power of forgiveness. Perhaps business success is the visible result that my client wants, but there is an invisible element that we need to resolve first.

Forgiveness is not about becoming so spiritual that you are able to forgive someone who has hurt you or wronged you in the past.

Forgiveness is the ability to recognize that someone has made a mistake, at a time when his or her mind was not aligned with love but with fear. In our most natural state, we are innocent and loving, but at that moment, he or she was not. Perhaps even for a long period of time, he or she chose everything but love. He or she didn't know any better but we do. We lean into the understanding that the person is capable of choosing something better despite the fact that he or she didn't. We forgive the person because we choose to see the innocence and love in that person, even if he or she could not see it. That doesn't mean what he or she did was acceptable when it isn't. The effect of the mistake is very real, but we are able to acknowledge the cause of the mistake and the true nature of the person. This is no simple task, forgiveness can be very difficult. The turning point is when you decide you are willing to go there.

Surrender or letting go is another concept that is sometimes misunderstood. This is not about giving up, throwing your hands in the air and saying, "I am done". It is about being clear what our heart wants, and that we have done what we are guided to do, and then relinquishing control of the outcome. It happens when we detach from what we want, especially the way in which we want something to happen or when we want it to happen. You cannot give what you don't have and you cannot have what you won't give. When we decide to finally let go of something or someone, we very often get the response we want or something even better. The universe is that miraculous.

Often when I think about who I need to forgive or what I need to surrender, the next thing that naturally comes to mind is gratitude. When we have forgiven someone or surrendered to a situation, we start to be able to see the silver lining or the lessons involved. There is always a blessing in disguise in every difficult situation, but the real challenge is to see what we can be grateful for. The more we feel grateful in life, the more there is to be grateful for.

**Essential Tool # 4**

*Whenever you feel sad, frustrated or worried, write down a minimum of three things that you feel grateful for in life.*

## Get inspired

Never stop learning. Pay attention to what interests you or inspires you and follow it. You will be amazed where it may lead. I cannot remember how I came across the subject matter of this book. It has elements of mythology, psychology and spirituality. I have read many books on these subjects through the years, but one day I started to have ideas about how they link together and how these concepts may be helpful to share with others. It was like a lamp was switched on. I have read many more books and studied the subject matter more deeply since then. I believe as human beings, we are naturally creative and imaginative. We need outlets to express ourselves, no matter whether it is in the form of creative art in the way the world defines it or simply through daily life. We need stimulation for our minds as well, we need new ideas or knowledge. It is like a circuit, in and out, that is when we feel most alive and life becomes more fun. So pick up a book or read a blog or listen to a podcast if you need some inspiring input, or think of something to express yourself to channel your creativity.

**Essential Tool # 5**

*Find your inspiration and follow your bliss.*

## DISCOVER YOUR DESTINY

You can discover your destiny by following your bliss, or you can ignore all the signs and detour from it. You have free will. In certain matters you must make a decision as the universe cannot force a choice upon you. You may be destined to become a bestselling author, but are you willing to write your book first? Or you may be meant to launch an innovation that will benefit many people in the world. Or you may be meant to be a wonderful mother. No destiny is too big or too small. It is our ride as spirit to experience being a human. No one can force you to do something great and meaningful, you will have to participate consciously in life, for yourself. If you are conscious and connected to your spiritual centre, which is your inner voice, you will be inspired by a story or certain subject matter, and you will naturally have the desire and ability to carry out your inspiration.

Many people have asked me how we may discern if we are truly inspired to do something or if it is our ego mind suggesting we should do it. The answer lies within you, no one else can answer for you. That is why regular spiritual practice such as meditation is so important, because it helps you to discern your truth. If you are inspired, you will feel energized and steady, you will also find help on the way. On the other hand, when you follow an ego-driven agenda, you will be motivated to do something by the fear of missing out, or of someone else taking advantage of the situation. If it is fear, it may be worry, envy or jealousy that is motivating your ego to do something. If it is inspired action, it usually comes from a central thought about serving others, helping the world. Thoughts of love feel very different to thoughts of fear.

If you are following your heart, the universe will be there to support you. The universe will never inspire you to do something and then leave you

alone. *The Course In Miracles* says there is no need to doubt the readiness of God, but only be aware of your own readiness. When you are ready, you will be called for your adventure. Your magical aid will appear. You will be summoned by your destiny to become who you are meant to be, just like a caterpillar is destined to become a butterfly. Your willingness is everything.

In the earlier chapters we learned about both the light and shadow aspects for each of the goddess archetypes. A strategic thinker like Athena may need to learn how to tune into her heart more. A passionate activist like Artemis may want to strengthen her connection with people. A carer-provider Demeter must be careful to avoid burnout, while Persephone must perhaps learn to trust herself more and be more assertive. We can all be charmed by a Hera because of who she is, not who she is married to, and she must know that too. As for Aphrodite, the most transformative of all, she needs to know her ability and use it for the greater good. It matters not which archetype is most active or dormant in you, what matters is knowing both your strengths and weaknesses, and acting wisely with integrity and grace. Use your heart as a moral compass and your intuition as a magical map. Set sail and go forth. You can never calculate the unknown, or predict the mysteries in life, so why not just enjoy the journey and be ready to be amazed.

The great poet Rumi wrote 'out beyond ideas of wrongdoing and rightdoing there is a field. I'll meet you there'. And I have came to learn that, beyond fear, we find love, above the ego we find our souls. There is a field connecting all of us. I'll meet you there.

# Next Steps

If you feel inspired or want some help with your transformational journey, join my reader list and you'll receive my bonus gifts and tools to support you. You will get access to my Goddess Archetypes Self-Assessment. This is a free online self-quiz that will give you a goddess profile and show you the most active or least active goddess influence in you right now.

By joining my reader list, you will also receive free meditation download, videos, audios, discount for my online courses during pre-launch period, invitations to my events and many more new gifts to come! Sign up at:

## www.SzeWingVetault.com/bonus

# Want to get coached?

If you would like to work with me 1-1 as your coach or consultant for your soul business, please email me via info@szewingvetault.com

***

If you found this book useful, I'd really appreciate a short review.

Your help in spreading the word is deeply appreciated and reviews make a huge difference in helping new readers find the book.

*A big 'Thank You' from my heart!*

# Endnotes

## Chapter 1

1. *The Goddess Within* by Jennifer Barker Woolger and Roger J. Woolger, pg. 7
2. *A Course In Miracles*, Foundation for Inner Peace, pg. 3
3. *A Woman's Worth,* Marianne Williamson, pg. 57-58
4. *The Hero with A Thousand Faces,* Joseph Campbell, pg. 49

## Chapter 2

5. *Goddesses - Mysteries of the Feminine Divine*, Joseph Campbell, pg. 15
6. *The Hero with a Thousands Faces*, Joseph Campbell, pg. 13
7. *Memories, Dreams, Reflections* Carl G. Jung, pg. 3
8. *Collective Works Vol. V*, Carl G. Jung, para. 244
9. *Collective Works Vol. V*, Carl G. Jung, para. 259
10. *Goddesses - Mysteries of the Feminine Divine*, Joseph Campbell, pg. 6
11. *The Goddess Within* by Jennifer Barker Woolger and Roger J. Woolger, pg. 7
12. *The Myth of Goddess - An Evolution of an Image* by Anne Baring and Jules Cashford, pg. 10-11
13. *Goddesses - Mysteries of the Feminine Divine*, Joseph Campbell, pg. 35

## Chapter 3

14. *The Homeric Hymns: Hymn to Athena,* translated by Jules Cashford, pg. 110

## Chapter 4

15. Extract from the Letter. Full quote can be found in *The Way of the Animal Powers,* Joseph Campbell, *pg.269.*
16. *The Homeric Hymns: Hymn to Artemis XXVII*, translated by Jules Cashford, pg. 133.

## Chapter 5

17. *Great quote from great leaders. Words from the leaders who shaped the world*, Peggy Anderson, pg. 12
18. *Goddesses - Mysteries of the Feminine Divine*, Joseph Campbell, pg. 3

## Chapter 6

N.A.

## Chapter 7

19. *Goddesses - Mysteries of the Feminine Divine*, Joseph Campbell, pg. 35
20. *Goddesses - Mysteries of the Feminine Divine*, Joseph Campbell, pg. xxii
21. *The Myth of Goddess - The Evolution of an Image* by Anne Baring and Jules Cashford. P 672-673
22. A quote from *Critique of Pure Reason* by Immanuel Kant

## Chapter 8

23. *The Homeric Hymns: Hymn to Aphrodite V*, translated by Jules Cashford, pg. 85

## Chapter 9

24. C.G. Jung, *The Portable Jung*, ed. Joseph Campbell, p.xxi

# Appendix 1: Aromatherapy and the Goddesses

### By Salvatore Battaglia

## Introduction

Initially I was a little challenged at the thought of explaining how to associate essential oils with the various goddesses. Dealing with essential oils for me is a very intuitive process and it is often difficult to explain my process of matching the essential oils to the goddess archetypes. Then it came to me – of course, my *Aroma Tree* is the perfect way to explain the associations.

As we relate different personality traits of the goddess archetypes to essential oils it is possible to see a recurring theme. In my *Aroma Tree* book (soon to be published) I examine the mythology and symbolism associated with each part of the *Aroma Tree* – the roots, wood, resin, flowers, leaves fruit and seeds.

The symbolism and myths associated with each part of the *Aroma Tree* help us understand the subtle and spiritual influences a plant may have. Our ancestors and many indigenous people around the world have long understood the deep spiritual connection we have with plants.

When we take time to reconnect with the stories and myths of our ancestors we enhance our spiritual connection with nature and the essential oils.

Have fun connecting with essential oils and learning how aromatherapy can help you tap into all your goddess archetypes.

# Roots

## Keywords
Grounded, mother nature, mysterious, tonic, earthy

## Essential oils
Essential oils from roots include angelica root, vetiver, spikenard and valerian. Essential oils from rhizomes (root stalks) include ginger, galangal and turmeric.

## Mythology & symbolism
In mythology roots are associated with our unconscious, mystery, the unknown, darkness, the power of nature and the quality of being unrefined. According to *The Book of Symbols*, roots are considered the "origin" or the "source". The English language uses the word root in "the root cause" or "the root of the problem". Symbolically roots also convey the idea of the tree-like process of growth, in which consciousness originates from the unconscious dimension of the psyche – the roots. The relationship with the unconscious is beautifully explained by Susanne Fischer-Rizzi when she describes vetiver, an essential oil that perfectly epitomizes root oils: "the scent of Mother Earth, mysteriously hidden in a deep, dark recess, drawing on the fullness of her life-giving energy."

## Goddess archetypes for essential oils from roots
Root oils – Demeter and Persephone
Rhizome oils – Athena

# Wood

## Keywords
Calm, courage, balance, focus, insight, protection, relaxation, serenity, sensitivity, strength, wisdom

## Essential oils
Wood oils are so precious. It takes decades for a plant to mature before a tree can be cut down to produce essential oils. Commonly used wood oils in aromatherapy include Atlas and Virginian cedarwood, guaicwood, *Santalum spicatum* and *Santalum album*.

(Please do not use any wood essential oils such as rosewood that are not sustainably grown as this leads to the destruction of native forests.)

## Mythology & symbolism
"When we think of wood we often think of trees and forests. They have a deep-rooted symbolic meaning in virtually all cultures. Forests represent the abode of nature spirits and trees are the guardians of nature spirits. The lion is to the animal kingdom, as the cedar is to the kingdom of trees. Majestic and full of strength, cedars stand tall in the loftiest regions of the mountains. They demand space for their expansive branches and stand undaunted by the elements in total inner harmony."

This description by Fisher-Rizzi of atlas cedarwood epitomises the strength, dignity and nobility that all trees have come to play in the human psyche.

Nancy Ross Hugo is the author of *Seeing Trees*, a beautiful book with breathtaking photographs of trees. She invites us to appreciate the vitality and beauty of trees. She says that because trees are often big and stationary, there is a tendency to think of them as monuments – impressive but inanimate. She says that because they are slow growing we often see them as symbols of fortitude and patience.

In mythology and symbolism words such as courage, eternity, immortality, longevity, nobility, strength and wisdom have been used to describe the characteristics of wood.

## Goddess archetypes for essential oils from wood
Artemis, Athena and Hera

# Resins

## Keywords
Healing, spiritually uplifting, purification on physical, emotional and spiritual planes, meditation, sacredness, spirituality

## Essential oils
The most commonly used resin oils in aromatherapy are frankincense and myrrh. I tend to classify resin oils into several groups:

- Sweet balsamic resins – benzoin, peru balsam.
- Rich, complex aromatic balsamic resins – rock rose (also known as cistus or labdanum), frankincense, myrrh and opoponax.
- Spicy balsamic resin – galbanum, elemi.

APPENDIX 1: AROMATHERAPY AND THE GODDESSES

## Mythology & symbolism

Resins such as benzoin, myrrh and frankincense are the oldest aromatic substances used by humankind. Resins were used as far back as 4,000 years ago as incense in religious ceremonies and fumigations by the ancient Egyptians.

Traditionally, resins were used as incense to ward off evil spirits. Frankincense and myrrh are mentioned in the bible as two of the three gifts the wise men gave to baby Jesus: 'And when they were come into the house, they saw the young child with Mary his mother, and fell down, and worshipped him: and when they had opened their treasures, they presented unto him gifts; gold, and frankincense, and myrrh.' (*Matthew 2:11*) These gifts symbolized his divinity and his status as a high priest, as frankincense was a key part of sacrifices to God in the Old Testament.

There are many theories regarding the symbolism of the three gifts of gold, frankincense and myrrh. All three gifts were considered offerings and gifts given to a king. Myrrh was commonly used as an anointing oil; frankincense as a perfume and gold as a valuable item. The three gifts also had a spiritual meaning: gold as a symbol of kingship on earth, frankincense as a symbol of divinity, and myrrh as an embalming oil and a symbol of death. Sometimes this is described more generally as gold symbolizing virtue, frankincense symbolizing prayer and myrrh symbolizing suffering.

## Goddess archetypes for essential oils from resin

Artemis and Persephone – all resin oils
Aphrodite – sweet resins

# Fruit

## Keywords
Creativity, abundance, enjoyment of life, purification, digestive system, lymphatic system

## Essential oils
Most of the fruit essential oils come from the rind of citrus fruits. I generally classify citrus fruit into two groups according to their aroma:

- Sweet citrus – sweet orange, mandarin.
- Sharp zesty citrus – grapefruit, lemon, cold-pressed lime, yuzu.

Bergamot is in a league of its own – it has a floral-fresh citrus aroma. Juniper berry oil is also classified as a fruit. While it does share many similar properties with the citrus oils, in our discussion of goddess archetypes juniper berry is more reminiscent of the conifer oils.

## Mythology & symbolism
In mythology fruits are often used as symbols of abundance. They are associated with pleasure, gluttony and temptation. They are also associated with fertility, youth and sensuality. Fruits are gifts from Mother Nature that provide us with nourishment. Throughout the Middle Ages fruit symbolizes good health.

For example, in Chinese tradition oranges signified a prayer or wish for good fortune. Fruit also symbolizes abundant happiness. When visiting family or friends during the New Year season it is customary to bring a gift of a bag of oranges or tangerines with the leaves still attached. This symbolizes the relationship between the giver and receiver of the gift, and shows that it is secure. If the gift is given to a newly married couple, it symbolizes the hope that the couple will be blessed with many children.

## Goddess archetypes for essential oils from fruit
Sharp citrus – Athena
Sweet citrus – Demeter and Aphrodite

# Seed

## Keywords
Change, growth, energy, creativity, spice

## Essential oils
When we think of seed oils it is usually a spicy aroma that comes to mind. Indeed most seed oils are used as spices. Commonly used seed oils in aromatherapy are aniseed, black pepper, caraway, cardamom, carrot seed, coriander seed, cumin, dill, fennel seed and nutmeg.

## Mythology & symbolism
In mythology seeds are often associated with nourishment, earthiness, reproduction, and the potential for growth. Just think about the size of a seed and the potential it holds. The seed is so small, it sits in the palm of your hand and yet it can grow into an incredible living structure. It can be stored for years and then given the right conditions, burst into life – a rich symbol of the process of living and dying.

## Goddess archetypes for essential oils from seed
Demeter and Aphrodite

# Leaf

## Keywords
Clarity, confidence, energy, focus, transformation, protection

## Essential oils
Leaf oils represent the largest and most diverse group of essential oils. It is easy to see a pattern once we group the leaf essential oils according to their origins. I like to classify leaf oils as those from:

- Herbs – essential oils such as basil, hyssop, sweet marjoram, melissa, peppermint, rosemary, thyme and sage.
- Trees – Camphoraceous including Australian oils such as eucalyptus and the melaleuca oils.
- Trees – Conifers including pine trees such as fir, hinoki, pine and spruce.
- Grasses – including citronella, lemongrass and palmarosa.

## Mythology & symbolism
In mythology, leaves have many different meanings. Generally leaves are symbolic of the cycles of death and renewal. When leaves are green they represent hope, renewal and revival. On the other hand, dead leaves represent decay and sadness. Leaves may also symbolize fertility and growth.

I love some of the ancient Greek myths regarding traditional herbs. Fischer-Rizzi explains the Greek myth of peppermint in the following tale: the Greek god Hades, ruler of the underworld, fell madly in love with a beautiful nymph, Mentha. His jealous wife, Persephone, pounded her to earth. Hades then turned poor Mentha into a wonderful healing fragrant plant that gave him some consolation.

Rosemary is another herb that was commonly used in ancient times. The Greeks and Romans considered rosemary a symbol of loyalty, death and remembrance. In the Middle Ages rosemary was thought to bring good luck and provide protection against magic and witchcraft.

## Goddess archetypes for essential oils from leaf

Athena – herbaceous leaf
Artemis – conifer leaf
Demeter – herbaceous leaf
Hera – camphoraceous leaf

# Flowers

## Keywords

Beauty, compassion, confidence, sensuality, sexuality, emotionally uplifting

## Essential oils

Of all the different plant structures, flowers are most fragrant, and the most delicate and expensive essential oils to make. I tend to classify flowers into three categories:

- Herbaceous florals – such as German and Roman chamomile, everlasting, clary sage, lavender.
- Light florals – such as rose otto, neroli.
- Rich heavy intoxicating florals – such as rose absolute, jasmine absolute, ylang ylang.

## Mythology & symbolism

The exquisite beauty and aroma of flowers are associated with so many myths and symbols – from life to death, purity to passion. Flowers are often associated with youth, beauty and pleasure; however as they wilt and die they represent impermanence and the fragility of life.

There is also something very sensual about flowers. It is not surprising because flowers are the sexual organs of the plant. Novelist Tom Robbins' description of Jasmine in his classic novel *Jitterbug Perfume*, describes the intense uplift and sensual nature of jasmine: "Ah, yes, leave it to jasmine to soothe the savage beast, for jasmine in its delightful way performs an olfactory pantomime of glad animal movements from times gone by. A few other flowers may be as sweet, but jasmine is sweet without sentiment, sweet without effeteness, sweet without compromise; it is aggressively sweet, outrageously sweet: 'I am sweet,' says jasmine, 'and if you don't like it, you can kiss my sweet ass. Expansive, yet never cloying; romantic, yet seldom melancholy."

The colours of flowers also have symbolic meaning. White blossoms for example represent purity and death, while red flowers often symbolize passion and energy and yellow represents gold or the sun.

The rose is compared to the soul by Sufi mystic, Hazrat Inayat Khanl. He describes the fragrance of a rose as the spiritual personality of the rose: "the soul becomes like a rose, and begins to show the rose quality. Just as the rose consists of many petals held together, so the person who attains to the unfoldment of the soul begins to show many different qualities. These qualities emit fragrance in the form of a spiritual personality. The rose has a beautiful structure and the personality which proves the unfoldment of the soul has a fine structure: in manner, in dealing with others, in speech, in action."

It is no wonder that Worwood describes the personality of rose otto as "one of gentleness and apparent perfection".

In Roman mythology, Flora was a goddess of flowers and the season of spring. While she was a minor figure in mythology she was one of the fertility goddesses. A festival in her honour was held annually and symbolized the renewal of the cycle of life, drinking and flowers.

## Goddess Archetypes for Essential Oils from Flower

Artemis and Hera – light florals
Demeter – herbaceous flowers
Persephone and Aphrodite – all flowers

# References

*A Course In Miracles* by Dr. Helen Schucman, 3rd edition published by Foundation for Inner Peace, 2008.

*A Woman's Worth* by Marianne Williamson, published by Random House USA Inc, 2003.

*Embracing the Goddess Within* by Kris Waldherr, published by Beyond Words Pub Co., 1997.

*Goddess Alive! Inviting Celtic & Norse Goddesses Into Your Life* by Michelle Skye and Illustrated by Kris Waldherr

*Goddesses and The Divine Feminine: A Western Religious History* by Rosemary Radford Ruether, published by University of California Press, Berkeley Los Angeles London.

*Goddesses in Everywoman: Powerful Archetypes in Women's Lives* by Jean Shinoda Bolen, MD. Anniversary edition published by HarperOne, 2009.

*Goddesses: Mysteries of Feminine Divine*, collected works of Joseph Campbell, published by New World Library 2004.

# REFERENCES

*Great Quotes from Great Leaders: Words from the Leaders Who Shaped the World* by Peggy Anderson, published by Simple Truths, 2017.

*Jung: A Very Short Introduction* by Antony Stevens, published by Oxford University Press, 2001.

*Man & His Symbols* edited by Carl G. Jung, published by Bantam Doubleday Dell Publishing Group Inc, 1999.

*Memories, Dreams, Reflection* by C.G. Jung, International Edition, published by HarperCollins Publishers, 1995.

*Myths to Live By: The Collective Works of Joseph Campbell* by Joseph Campbell, 2nd edition published by Joseph Campbell Foundation, 2011.

*Pathway to Bliss: Mythology and Personal Transformation* by Joseph Campbell, published by New World Library 2004.

*The Book of Goddesses: Expanded Anniversary Edition* by Kris Waldherr, published by Art and Words Editions, 2010.

*The Goddess Within: A Guide to the Eternal Myths That Shape Women's Lives* by Jennifer Barker Woolger and Roger J. Woolger, published by Ballantine Books, 1989.

*The Hero With a Thousand Faces* by Joseph Campbell, 3rd edition published by New World Library, 2015.

*The Hero's 2 Journeys* by Michael Hauge and Christopher Vogler (Audio Program)

*The Homeric Hymns* by Homer, published by Penguin Classics, 2003.

*The Myth of the Goddess : Evolution of an Image* by Anne Baring and Jules Cashford, published by Penguin Books Ltd, 1993.

*The Odyssey* by Homer (Amazon Classics Edition)

*The Portable Jung* by C.G. Jung, edited by Joseph Campbell, published by Penguin Books, 1977.

*The Power of Myth* by Joseph Campbell and Bill Moyers, published by Bantam Doubleday Dell Publishing Group Inc, 1991.

*The Women's Wheel of Life* by Elizabeth Davis and Carol Leonard, published by Bad Beaver Publishing, 2012.

Women Who Run with Wolves: Myths and Stories of the Wild Woman Archetype by Clarissa Pinkola Estes, published by Random House USA Inc. 1997.

# About Sze Wing

Sze Wing Vetault is a coach, author and creative entrepreneur specializing in personal development and spirituality. A graduate of The London School of Economics and Political Science, she began her career as an economist and later worked as a consultant. Sze Wing takes a practical and holistic approach to personal and business transformation. She coaches individuals and purpose-driven businesses to inspire change and foster growth. Sze Wing has presented her work in Australia and overseas. She is also a co-founder of the Lighten Up™ Summit; an online video summit showcasing Australian conscious thought leaders in the health & wellness industry.

A native of Hong Kong, Sze Wing spent 7 years living in Europe before moving to Australia. She lives in Sydney with her husband Bastien and daughter Olivia. Sze Wing enjoys travelling as often as possible. She loves dancing, yoga and tea. Her favorite topics to read or discuss are spirituality, mythology, psychology, scientific discoveries and ancient civilizations.

*Connect with Sze Wing online:*
**Facebook.com/CoachSzeWing**
**Twitter.com/CoachSzeWing**

*You will find her blogs, videos, podcasts, online courses and free eBooks on her website:*
**www.SzeWingVetault.com**

# Acknowledgement

Dedicated, with gratitude, to all those writers who have impacted my life with their inspirational books.

Thanks to everyone who completed my goddess archetypes assessment and those who encouraged me to take on the path of creating this book.

Special thanks to Salvatore Battaglia at Perfect Potion for being a tremendous contributor and mentor.

Thanks to Monique Perrine at Nettlesoup for editing, to Suzana Stankovic at LSD Design for the book cover, Karen Koski at Whimsical Muse for the goddess images and the folks at Book Cover Café for the interior design, typesetting and formatting.

Thanks to Julia Tritsaris and Marie Tritsaris for their kind and generous support at the 11th hour.

Last but not least, my dear husband Bastien Vetault for covering me at home and supporting my endeavor in so many ways.

www.ingramcontent.com/pod-product-compliance
Lightning Source LLC
Chambersburg PA
CBHW062058290426
44110CB00022B/2637